IMRAN KHAN

A SEASONED POLITICIAN

EMILY

CONTENTS

IMRAN KHAN: THE GOAT

(GREATEST OF ALL TIME)

"The success of Mr. Khan's party upended the decades-old political playbook governing Pakistan, a nuclear-armed nation of 240 million. Throughout those years, the military has wielded ultimate authority, guiding its politics behind a veil of secrecy, and civilian leaders have typically risen to power only with its support — or been driven from office by its heavy hand.

The vote also showed that Mr. Khan's strategy of preaching reform and railing against the military has resonated deeply with Pakistanis — particularly young people — who are disillusioned with the political system. It also proved that his loyal base of supporters was seemingly immune to the military's old tactics for demoralizing voters, including arresting supporters and issuing long prison sentences to their political leaders days before the vote."

— THE NEW YORK TIMES (2024)

"What's happening to Imran Khan right now is both ridiculous & outrageous. It makes Pakistan a laughing stock to the rest of the world. And the fact that Western countries are silent as such moves are made speaks volumes about our leaders' empty rhetoric about protecting democracy."

— MEHDI HASAN ON X FORMERLY TWITTER (2024)

"Pakistan's Prime Minister Imran Khan has emerged as the 9th most popular world leader with over 9.4 million followers on social networking website Twitter.

The premier is at the 9th most followed world leaders on Twitter, according to Spectator Index, a website that displays statistics and international rankings from the fields of politics, economics, history, military affairs, sports, science and technology."

— GULF TODAY (2019)

"Even though the 71-year-old is barred from running in the 8 February general election, he continues to be a powerful force dividing the Muslim majority country. For some of its 240 million population, he is an anti-establishment hero."

— BBC NEWS (2024)

"He rode to power in 2018 on a populist platform promising social reforms, religious conservatism and a fight against corruption, overturning decades of rule by two feuding political dynasties interspersed with military takeovers."

— FRANCE 24 (2022)

"Former cricketing superstar Khan enjoys enormous support in Pakistan, but his campaign of defiance against the powerful military establishment, which spread through the nation after his ouster, has met with a fierce backlash.

Pakistan's military has directly ruled the country for roughly half of its 76-year history, and continues to exercise enormous power."

— ARAB NEWS (2023)

"The actions taken against former prime minister Imran Khan's political party in recent months followed a familiar playbook for a disgraced political movement in Pakistan. Khan was jailed on charges that his supporters say were politically motivated, party offices were raided, and its election efforts were ignored by TV networks."

— THE WASHINGTON POST (2024)

"The arrest of former Prime Minister of Pakistan, Imran Khan, is a dark day for democracy," he tweeted."

— ALJAZEERA (2023)

"Driven by fierce ambition, he can be cold and calculating. But he still generates the broadest hope among young and old that he can turn Pakistan around, and help make South Asia an ocean of peace rather than a state of permanent conflict."

— TIME MAGAZINE

DEAR READERS,

I am honoured to share with you my analytical work: "Imran Khan -a Seasoned Politician" -impartially chronicling the extraordinary personal and political journey of one of Pakistan's most impactful national leaders.

Given the deeply polarised views dominating public discourse lately around Khan's bold opposition towards the ex-coalition regime, I felt that an objective narrative grounded in historical facts, free of sensationalism, could provide thoughtful citizens and youth the necessary perspective to independently evaluate his legitimacy as a serious political challenger. Too much commentary these days loses nuance in partisan shouting matches. My father taught me that genuine wisdom resides in pausing to understand context and investigate truth. All leaders deserve fair critique but also credit where changes for the good manifest. So I trace Khan's gradual evolution based on his own words and objectively observable milestones over four decades in the spotlight.

The biography covers substantive ground that few contemporary analyses attempt, due to the conventional rush to react to headlines of the day. We examine his beginnings as a x | *Dear Readers,*

shy child in privileged circumstances where fame first
beckoned for him as a mercurial sports prodigy, through Khan's
spectacular cricket captaincy years turning him into a global
icon, then the extraordinary mid-career shift into mass-scale
philanthropy. That eventually became the springboard to
embarking on his audacious new quest targeting the highest
governance office through an idealistic reform agenda.

I invite readers to closely study Khan's record since, the
consistency of his anti-corruption focus and grassroots
engagement trying to transform a cynical political structure
dominated by family dynasties, and wealthy electable and
patronage sycophants.

Unlike leaders who make idealistic promises prior to
elections but struggle to maintain those principles once in
office, Khan has focused consistently on anti-corruption
reforms despite initially limited popular momentum behind
such platforms. He further risked early support by taking
controversial stands against militancy, even when unpopular
with right-wing bases.

His welfare, justice and accountability initiatives achieved
notable traction in many areas, though the ultimate impact
remains unfinished, given his abbreviated tenure. Khan's
defiance of the current authority's democratic legitimacy and
the allegations of creeping totalitarianism, driving protests
demanding early elections, require deeper analysis. Some
question the wisdom in terms of consequences to stability,
while supporters applaud his bold refusal to accept restrictions
on dissent.

Ultimately, reasonable minds may draw different inferences
regarding his achievements or controversies as ex-prime
minister. But the intentions manifesting through a singular
focus over four decades in public life appear remarkably
consistent and sincere. In a landscape littered with petty
opportunists and insincere figureheads, Khan's idealistic

perseverance demands serious attention whether or not one agrees with his diagnoses and solutions entirely.

My purpose is not hagiography but offering insight into his motivations, sacrifice, and frequent swimming against the tide that makes his journey as a national leader rather extraordinary. The reader can determine his subsequent credibility. I welcome healthy public debate, as my late father taught -for in the open sharing of perspectives without malice lies societal progress.

'ABSOLUTELY NOT!'

WHY I CHOOSE IMRAN KHAN AS MY LEADER

Imran Khan is a prominent figure in Pakistan's political landscape. Before entering politics, he had a successful career as a cricket player, captaining the Pakistan national cricket team to a World Cup victory in 1992. He founded the Pakistan Tehreek-e-Insaf (PTI) political party in 1996, which aimed to promote justice, anti-corruption measures, and better governance in Pakistan. Over the years, Imran Khan gained popularity for his bold stance against external influence on Pakistan's sovereignty, and for his advocacy for the rights of Palestinians and Kashmiris.

Imran Khan's charismatic personality and dedication to social causes have garnered support from many Muslims around the world. His willingness to address issues such as Islamophobia on international platforms, like the United Nations, has been praised by his followers.

Imran Khan was elected as prime minister of Pakistan in July 2018, after his party Pakistan Tehreek-e-Insaf (PTI) emerged victorious in the general elections. Khan served as prime minister of Pakistan for nearly four years, before being ousted in April 2022 through a no-confidence vote in

Parliament -becoming the first democratically elected PM to be removed in this manner. While Khan was not the first prime minister to be removed while in office, he was the first democratically elected PM to be removed specifically through a no-confidence vote in Pakistan's National Assembly. Previous prime ministers, like Zulfikar Ali Bhutto and Nawaz Sharif, were removed in the 1970s and 1990s through mechanisms like presidential dismissal and military coups rather than no-confidence votes while in office. So while Khan's removal continues a pattern of political instability in Pakistan, the use of a legislative no-confidence vote makes his dismissal historically unique among democratically elected prime ministers in the country.

After Imran Khan's removal as prime minister, the government of Pakistan, backed by the military establishment, filed nearly 200 controversial cases against him. On 9 May 2023, Khan was arrested inside a courtroom in Islamabad, and later, in August 2023, he was arrested from his residence in Lahore. Khan is still in prison as I'm writing this book. Notably, Khan was also a victim of an attack on 3 November 2022, when he was shot, but miraculously survived.

However, Imran Khan's recent imprisonment, held on baseless charges, sparked admiration among his supporters. They believe that his resilience and his refusal to back down in the face of adversity reflect strong leadership qualities. For many seeking courageous Muslim leaders, figures like Khan and Turkey's President Recep Tayyip Erdoğan hold appeal. Devoted followers of Khan have even created merchandise and decorated the walls of their restaurants across the world branded with Khan's viral "Absolutely Not!" statement and "Prisoner No. 804", the number allotted to Imran Khan during his imprisonment at Attock jail, Pakistan.

For Khan's ardent supporters, his words and actions carry weight and symbolism. While critiques and dissent also exist,

Khan has cultivated a devoted following for the values and resistance he represents to them. His supporters are drawn to different aspects of his vision, rhetoric, and policies, based on their individual principles and beliefs. Throughout history, certain leaders have had an almost mystical ability to inspire devotion in their followers. Their extraordinary charisma and vision can profoundly influence people, beyond typical popularity. In contemporary times, figures like actor Shah Rukh Khan and footballer Cristiano Ronaldo command dedicated fan bases globally.

Entrepreneur Elon Musk has cultivated an intensely loyal following for his visionary leadership in electric vehicles and space exploration. Politician Bernie Sanders galvanised a grassroots movement around progressive policies and bold stances on issues like healthcare and education. Musician and philanthropist Paul David Hewson (known as Bono) uses his platform to inspire activism around social causes like poverty and disease prevention. Spiritual leader Jagadish Vasudev, famous as Sadhguru, builds community around practices of inner wellbeing and self-transformation. Though across different domains, the magnetism and the messages of leaders continue to deeply resonate with many in the modern era.

In the political sphere, some leaders, like Muhammad Ali Jinnah, the founder of Pakistan, have gained such national reverence that citizens are ready to passionately serve their country's cause. Similarly, Zulfikar Ali Bhutto's populist leadership galvanised mass public support in his era. Figures who earn such widespread veneration are rare. My leader is one amongst such great leaders.

While many notable leaders exist, the degree of voluntary, grassroots zeal among followers separates truly iconic figures from the rest. However, we must be cautious about excessive idolisation of any individual. Measured, critical analysis should balance acknowledgement of exceptional leadership qualities, with recognition that all leaders are human and flawed.

Personally, I find myself deeply inspired by Imran Khan for reasons elaborated upon in this book. However, treating any political figure as infallible risks blind allegiance. Wisdom lies in uplifting the universal values leaders embody at their best, while still questioning authority constructively as engaged citizens. If insightfully harnessed, inspiration can unite people behind progress, while avoiding personality cults.

This book details the reasons why I personally choose Imran Khan as a leader who inspires me. The book highlights an important dimension that amplifies its unique value - including perspectives of passionate grassroots supporters powering Khan's movement, challenging status quo exploitation. Their authentic voices matter greatly, despite lacking prominent profiles, since these courageous, ordinary citizens bear the brunt of misgovernance under corrupt regimes.

Initially, I sought interviews with high-visibility members within Khan's party to incorporate insider insights. However, some remained inaccessible, given their hectic political responsibilities or their wariness towards an unknown first-time author lacking personal access. These limitations frustratingly resemble the systemic barriers we critique obstructing meritocracy! But counsel from senior lawyer Naeem Haider Panjutha helped rediscover what Khan has embodied his entire career -prioritising ordinary citizens over entitled elites when judging visionary potential or moral resilience. Our supposed elders in privilege repeatedly betray, while selfless students, farmers, and workers display people's powerful potency through sacrifices for reform. Their participation gave birth to PTI as a conduit for marginalised masses to reclaim democratic rights. They sustain its mission today as the freedom of movement against authoritarianism.

These unsung warriors always spur Khan onwards while entitled spectators chase compromise. Hence, this work shifts focus to amplifying voices of common Pakistanis powering the "Haqiqi Azadi". Readers would gain a grassroots perspective regarding what compels their phenomenal loyalty towards Khan's cause, spanning over two generations now. From youth rejecting dynastic cabals to mothers praying for resistance victory over tyranny,-their stories must resound loudly to inspire the hesitant that ending servility remains possible!

I owe deep gratitude towards Imran Khan's lawyer, Naeem Haider Panjutha, for his guidance, and to the selfless PTI volunteers who have enriched this book with their vital perspectives from the grassroots. Their generosity with time and willingness to share personal journeys has made this collaborative endeavour more impactful.

The inclusion of diverse citizens' voices across ages, genders, and socioeconomic backgrounds added much needed richness, nuance and versatility to the analysis. Rather than limiting commentary to a single homogeneous narrative perspective, we get to hear directly from ordinary Pakistanis driving the reform agenda through individual sacrifices. Their trust in opening up intimately about motivations, struggles, and dreams for a more just Pakistan injects these pages with profound emotional resonance and raw authenticity no expert commentary alone could match.

By profiling students suspended for activism, farmers losing lifelong land without recompense, mothers praying for arrested daughters or sons, and elderly artists creating subversive art against state repression, each co-author from civil society helps illustrate the myriad oppressions that unite a rainbow resistance under Imran Khan's leadership. Their stories lucidly capture ground realities driving outrage against governance failing basic welfare and rights. Together, their narratives woven amongst my own, elevate this chronicle beyond a political biography and towards almost a people's oral history underscoring why, for them, Khan signifies singular hope.

Had I interviewed only prominent elites or academic figures, this work would lack the necessary diversity of situations, tone, and texture. The grassroots voices manifest the beating heart powering a movement long dismissed as marginal. As Khan repeats, the mango people now determine their own destiny, not remote aristocrats. It was a privilege to provide a publishing platform to overlooked co-authors representing the masses finally rising to reclaim an unfulfilled nationhood. Through their courage and aspirations lies Pakistan's redemption. Their souls shine within these pages.

THE ROOTS OF MY VOICE
FAMILY, CONVICTION, AND IMRAN KHAN'S INSPIRATION

Unlike most of my family, I'm not simply a people-pleaser who agrees to everything. From my father, I gained the urge to question traditions handed down that may be flawed. However, like many women (and even men) raised in certain societies, I struggle with an ingrained fear of disrupting expectations by asserting my own needs. This makes me want to challenge unjust societal norms, yet I feel guilt and self-blame for inconveniencing others with my disagreement. I try to overcome those fears so I can use my voice to spark positive change, even if it means questioning deeply-rooted standards that others follow without debate. With practice, I know I can find the right balance, challenging dated mindsets while still showing care and consideration in my approach. Questioning the status quo requires courage, but it is necessary for progress.

Questioning the status quo also requires true grit and unwavering conviction. I'm fortunate to have my father's example to inspire my own resolute spirit. He remained steadfast in his beliefs, even as others criticised him. Weathering criticism with determination ultimately earned his adversaries' respect. My leader, Imran Khan's fearless persistence against disapproval also deeply motivates me. Of course, braving consequences for dissent is never easy. But acquiescing to please the judgemental masses means forsaking one's purpose. My father's life taught me that living with courage and principle, though difficult, is infinitely more rewarding than spineless conformity.

Should anyone subordinate their own morals to appease the status quo? Our ancestors were equally human, equally flawed. Progress demands that we challenge even supposed wisdom passed down. A life lived solely from obligation seems woefully hollow and wasted. I believe each of us has a purpose:-to improve both self and society. Like my leader, I aim to inspire others more by deed than word. Naturally, such conviction incites criticism from those invested in upholding tradition. Yet pursuing a higher purpose provides a far deeper fulfilment than fleeting public opinion ever could. True freedom lies in steadfastly abiding by one's principles, not the fickle expectations of others. My leader understands this, finding meaning in adversity because it advances us toward justice. Conforming for acceptance may be easier, but a life of courageous conviction, however uncomfortable at times, is infinitely more enriching.

True leadership requires challenging prevailing norms for positive change. History respects those who questioned unjust systems, whether secular or religious. The Prophet Muhammad, peace be upon him, denounced idol worship and mistreatment of the vulnerable. Jesus Christ upended common practices of corruption and materialism among religious elites. More recently, Mahatma Gandhi challenged imperialism through nonviolence. Nelson Mandela opposed apartheid from prison. My leader confronts injustice through principled dissent. Though the easy path is silence, leaders give a voice to the oppressed. They understand that steering society toward justice is worth adversity. While sycophants may temporarily appease power structures, enlightened leaders focused on reform leave an enduring legacy.

While famous figures can inspire, role models exist among friends and family, too. But inspiration requires humility -a willingness to accept wisdom, even from unexpected sources. Our egos often hinder us from recognising lessons around us, trapping us in jealousy or insecurity instead. Yet the human urge to learn and improve can prevail, if we quiet our need for comparison and control. Openness to opposing views is difficult but essential for growth. As a child, my father taught me conviction not through grand acts, but subtle, daily choices guided by integrity. The wisest teachers patiently mentor more by listening than lecturing. Aspiration need not breed unhealthy competition. If we release our assumptions, inspiration flows freely from anyone committed to progress, regardless of worldly status. By opening our mind's eye to the humanity in all, we can find inspiration almost anywhere we choose to seek it.

Without positive inspiration, people can fall prey to those spreading messages of hatred. Siblings compared unfavourably can internalize deep insecurities, ripe for manipulation. Much suffering stems from such festering envy. Demagogues exploit these feelings of weakness, channelling rage toward scapegoats.

Nationalism has stoked horrific violence throughout history. The demonisation of Tutsis enabled Rwanda's genocide. Nazi Germany arose from wounded German pride after the first world war. Even now, extremists capitalise on disenfranchised people whose identities feel threatened.

The rage and insecurity of leaders has fuelled the ongoing tragedies in Ukraine and Palestine, causing immense suffering for civilians. However, figures like Mahatma Gandhi and Martin Luther King Jr. showed the power of dignity and hope. A society uplifting the downtrodden can redirect youth away from destruction. No child is born hateful -they learn it from elders poisoned by cynicism.

By being the change, mentoring the lost, and believing in human potential, we can break these cycles, as my own leader strives to do through his message of empowerment and justice for all people. With enough sparks of light, darkness can be overcome.

As a nonconformist, I've faced disapproval for my willingness to question the status quo. Yet had I conformed, I wouldn't have become who I am. While difficult, living authentically provides an inner satisfaction that people-pleasing cannot match.

My mother, bless her, chose a more submissive path, lacking role models to embolden her dissent. But as parents, our duty extends beyond our lives alone. We must equip our children to achieve what we could not, empowering them to fearlessly make this world more just, even if they question our own beliefs in the process.

Parenting courageously means accepting that our children may outgrow our mindsets. It requires grappling with difficult questions that shake our foundations but which strengthen theirs. The greatest gift we can give is confidence in their ability to think independently and create positive change.

My mother gave me life; my father, conviction. By combining those gifts, I can breathe new life and conviction into my community. With courage and compassion, we can plant seeds today that will blossom into fruits we may not live to see. But our children's children will look back gratefully at our efforts.

There is no higher purpose than empowering the next generation. Parenting well takes perseverance, humility, and farsightedness. We must look beyond ourselves, ignoring critics stuck in their ways. The future rests in brave young hands. Our job is simply to hand them the torch, then get out of their light.

I wish to honour Shaukat Khanum, the late mother of Imran Khan, for instilling the integrity and strength of character that helped shape her son into the leader he is today. It is often caring yet courageous parenting that empowers children to achieve greatly.

However, circumstances can also impart formative lessons, even in the absence of parents. The Prophet Muhammad, peace be upon him, was orphaned at a young age, yet demonstrated resilience and wisdom beyond his years. Through the hardships he endured, the Prophet developed extraordinary compassion and fortitude.

So while good parenting plays a crucial role, the fire of adversity can also forge strong leaders. With wise guidance and access to knowledge, even the least privileged child may rise up to enlighten society. The human spirit can shine radiantly, if given loving nourishment and room to grow. Take the Khan family, for instance. Shaukat Khanum instilled integrity in her children, though she lacked higher education herself. Imran excelled as a cricketer before entering politics. His sisters, Aleema, Rubina, and others pursued higher studies, yet demonstrate the same virtues as those their mother imprinted.

Family bonds build character regardless of privilege. Cristiano Ronaldo grew up poor in Portugal, completing only primary studies. Yet his natural competitive spirit, honed playing with his siblings, fuelled the drive that led him to football stardom.

Educational opportunities amplify natural talents but are not their source. With passion and work ethic, even those without academic credentials can achieve greatness. The key is nurturing one's innate gifts.

When families unite behind purpose, trials temper their values. Shaukat's children stand steadfastly by Imran Khan, the sisters fighting cases to defend their brother. Their devotion shows family comes first.

If we hope to uplift humanity, these lessons need imparting across generations. With wisdom binding families, virtue can bloom despite adversity. It starts at home, with parental roots thriving only when nourished by siblings' support.

Certain qualities consistently define extraordinary leaders - those rare individuals who alter the tide of history. By studying inspiring examples - from my father to current leaders to legendary figures worldwide - I aim to distil the core human attributes that enabled their monumental success.

In the chapters ahead, I will examine key traits like unwavering integrity, raw courage, resilience through adversity, boundless compassion, and visionary and strategic thinking. My goal is to uncover the timeless human virtues and mindsets that rise above circumstance to drive positive change, regardless of context or ideology.

While the particular struggles these leaders confronted differed greatly, deeper shared characteristics unite them in purpose and principle. By chronicling my own observations and reflections, I hope to elucidate these universal traits, motivations and behaviours to inspire current and future generations.

True leadership begins inside each of us. If we can nurture these seeds of human potential --both individually and collectively --we too may leave an uplifting, enduring legacy. The great leaders of ages past continue shining as beacons so that we may also find light within ourselves.

My inspiration stems from gratitude --to my extraordinary role models in my late father and Imran Khan, and to my family, whose encouragement fuels my drive. I am blessed with children, whose trust motivates me to embark on projects like this book to lead an impactful life. I am grateful for my beautiful mother and my family's unwavering support through their prayers for my success. My family's strength gives me the foundation to take on ambitious endeavours.

I also wish to thank the passionate volunteers of PTI's social media team. Like keyboard warriors, they work tirelessly to amplify my leader's voice online against all odds. And to the frontline warriors and foot soldiers, thank you for putting service above self to walk the talk of principled leadership.

I want to offer my deepest gratitude to Madiha Ahmad and the entire UK SMT volunteer team for their invaluable efforts, enabling me to publish this book. Madiha went above and beyond --spearheading fundraising campaigns, arranging impactful interviews, and mobilising resources and platforms to promote my message. It was through the team's relentless commitment of time, energy and passion towards the shared goals of truth and justice that I was empowered to write freely. This book is a testament to what civic participation can achieve even in the face of censorship. Groups like UK SMT amplify voices that would otherwise be suppressed. Their selfless community organising fuels movements much larger than themselves. I sincerely appreciate all the volunteers for giving towards a cause greater than themselves and for making my book a reality when the freedom to publish uncensored stories hangs under threat.

Through my journey, I have gained a deep appreciation for the qualities of courage, resilience, compassion and integrity that define great leaders. I feel compelled to chronicle Imran Khan's story to preserve his legacy for generations to come. By extracting lessons from visionary figures worldwide, I hope this book helps cultivate strong leadership in our youth. My father gave me the vision to recognise noble leadership. Now I endeavour to pay that gift forward, empowering others to embrace the leader within.

1

"LA ILAHA ILLALLAH"

FAITH IN THE ONENESS OF ALLAH

The simplicity of "La ilaha illallah" masks its gravity for Muslims. In one poetic utterance, the essence of Islamic theology is crystallized. To proclaim "There is no god but Allah" is to embrace the singular perfection and sovereignty of the Divine. Besides Allah, none merit total obedience or reverence. This uncompromising monotheism forms the bedrock of Muslim belief. Yet "La ilaha illallah" alone is incomplete. For full resonance, it must be paired with "Muhammadun rasool Allah." Only together do these form the Kalimah Tayyibah -the Declaration of Faith.

With the addition of "Muhammad is the Messenger of Allah," devotion to the Prophet joins reverence for the Creator. Following the way of Muhammad (PBUH) becomes critical for worshipping properly and living righteously. By sincerely avowing the full Kalimah, Muslims cement the Oneness of God and the guidance of His greatest emissary. This statement may be quiet prayer or jubilant refrain, but its meaning remains mighty. In few words, it maps the path of Islamic faith -turning away from all false deities and honouring the Prophet who completed Allah's message. For those who truly take it to heart, the Kalimah instils purpose, direction and freedom. At its essence, proclaiming the Oneness of Allah fosters powerful virtues in believers. Total devotion to the Divine spurns submission to any worldly being. Remembering that all perishes except Allah nurtures humility, subduing egoism.

But today, even in deeply religious communities like mine, such rock-solid belief in "La ilaha illallah" is scarce. Though mosques and seminaries proliferate here in my Peshawar village, internalising faith appears absent.

Rituals endure, prayers are offered, sermons attended. Yet the soul-transforming ethos fuelling these acts has somehow been drained away. The motions continue, but conviction has withered. Mouthing "La ilaha illallah" no longer anchors people in purpose and restraint. Emptied of meaning, it offers no resistance against bending to false idols -wealth, power, nationalism, self-interest. Without its animating force, faith becomes hollow rigidity.

What I feel a few of us today is reconnecting with the animating spirit behind "La ilaha illallah." In our community, often the form of faith persists but its inner fire has cooled. Yet we once understood that proclaiming Divine Oneness anchored life in purpose and humility.

I wonder how we can relearn the awe and gratitude that come from perceiving Allah's peerless majesty. How to again let this profound realisation infuse moral strength into our hearts and commitments.

In an era where true devotion has diminished, leaders like Imran Khan stand apart in their steadfast embodiment of "La ilaha illallah." Steering free of worshipping false idols and upholding strength of character, Imran Khan mirrors reformers of the past who revived Islamic principles in decadent times. Looking back through history reveals the recurrent struggle of balancing faith with earthly temptations. In pre-Islamic Arabia, practices like female infanticide, usury and idolatry were rampant amidst tribalism and vengeance. During the Umayyad dynasty, corruption seeped back into the ruling class. In the late Abbasid period, extravagance and worldliness led to neglect of religion.

So too today, an obsession with wealth, power and nationalism has led our ummah astray. But just as courageous voices pulled believers back in previous eras, we too have reformist leaders reminding us of what "La ilaha illallah" truly entails --integrity, justice, modesty and purpose.

Figures like Imran Khan demonstrate that living by one's principles is possible, even when surrounded by compromise. By submitting wholly to Allah's commands rather than personal interests or public pressure, he upholds the Prophets' way. His example serves as a compass directing us back to true monotheistic belief.

Like many, I once thought regular mosque attendance was the mark of a good Muslim. But my late father opened my eyes. He saw that too often, preachers lectured about morality yet neglected justice and compassion in their own communities. My father refused to pray at our local mosque, but preferred praying at home mostly. He asked why sermons fixated on ritualism but ignored real ethics like women's rights, caring for orphans, equality for minorities. He wanted religion to uplift society, not divide it.

Controversially, he argued that men doing Tableegh for months inflicted harm by abandoning families without support. He believed faith manifests in small, daily acts of righteousness, not grand shows of piety.

My father drew from Islam's universal principles -justice, dignity, mercy. He exemplified these through selfless community service, reminding that all are deserving of respect and care, regardless of gender, status or belief.

While his opinions made him unpopular with traditionalists, I will always admire my father's willingness to point out hypocrisy and risk censure for speaking truth. He taught me that genuine faith expresses itself through courage, compassion and conscience, not empty words and hollow rituals.

In an era of superficial religious displays, Imran Khan represents a rare kind of principled leadership. His vision for reform connects to Islam's early figures, like Umar bin Abdul Aziz, who led by uplifting society's morals and welfare.

Today, too many exploit religion for power and privilege rather than social justice. Behind choreographed shows of piety - flowing beards, raised shalwars, impassioned sermons - corruption and indifference to inequality fester. Contrast this with the Prophet's humility, ethics and devotion to the marginalised.

Imran Khan does not benefit from theatrics. For him, faith manifests through tireless advocacy for reforming unjust structures and elevating the vulnerable. His life demonstrates that leadership is not about posturing, but aligning one's actions with Islamic ideals of justice, accountability and human dignity.

Cynics question why a clean-shaven cricket star champions these timeless values. But progress flows from character and conviction, not appearance. Imran Khan perseveres because his commitment to serve the people comes from within, from true belief, not external validation. His path follows the Prophet's struggle against vested interests for social justice. Where most leaders appease the powerful, Imran Khan confronts privilege and corruption unequivocally. Where it is tempting to ignore injustice, he raises his voice for the voiceless. Where insecurity breeds despots, he remains accountable to the people.

This reformer's spirit harkens back to early caliphs like Umar ibn Abdul Aziz. But for too long, our memory has faded. Imran Khan resurrects this enlightened model because he recognises that reforming the state creates lasting positive impact. Despite obstacles, he persists in this vision for change.

In an age of cynicism, Imran Khan reaffirms that faith, combined with wisdom and compassion, can uplift nations. Not faith that manifests in chants and garb, but faith that flows into justice, temperance and selfless public service. If we wish to progress, we must revive this true spirit of religion. Imran Khan's steadfast devotion to "La ilaha illallah" poses a formidable threat to powerful forces accustomed to deference. They have marshalled the full might of their influence and resources to coerce him into submission -hundreds of false legal cases, imprisonment and mistreatment, brazen attacks on his life, persecution of his loved ones, including the illegal abduction of his nephew, Hassan Niazi.

Yet nothing has succeeded in shaking Imran Khan's resolve, fortified by faith. His unwavering belief in the Divine has rendered him impervious, willing to endure any worldly trial in defence of truth and justice. He persists in speaking out against corruption and inequality, no matter the consequences. While ordinary politicians bow readily to safeguard their privilege, Imran Khan bows only to the commands of Allah and the moral code enshrined in Islam. His enemies have realised that no coercion, bribery or threat will ever make him abandon this mission to reform a broken system. And this refusal to compromise has unleashed their fury.

So they resort to demonising a rare leader who respects no authority above justice and accountability. But the determination instilled in Imran Khan by "La ilaha illallah" continues inspiring millions disenchanted with the status quo. His steadfast adherence reminds that with sincere faith comes fearlessness, integrity and sense of purpose.

By resisting unrelenting pressure, Imran Khan sets an outstanding example of resilience and commitment to reform for the greater public good. Indeed, the greatest test of faith is remaining unflinching when confronted with adversity and injustice. Imran Khan lifts his head high, placing full trust in the Divine plan as he walks this difficult path.

What truly irks his detractors is Imran Khan's refusal to play by the rules of elite privilege and patronage. He appeals directly to the Pakistani people, upholding their right to liberty from dynastic kleptocracy. And this promise of People Power threatens those few who have long subverted democracy for personal gain. But Imran Khan also represents the best of enlightened Muslim leadership -the spirit of justice, accountability and faith embodied by Islam's early reformist leaders. He understands that reforming the state creates lasting positive impact for the citizenry. Come what may, Imran Khan remains committed to this vision for change.

In the age of cynicism and morally bankrupt politics, Imran Khan reaffirms that faith, combined with wisdom, courage and compassion can uplift nations from seemingly insurmountable challenges. His life exemplifies redemption through trying sincerely to walk the righteous path.

My father bravely stood up for our rights against patriarchal norms, ensuring his daughters received education despite opposition. He was a pillar protecting us from threats. Yet had persecution come from the powerful state, I cannot say if he would have persisted. Perhaps he may have surrendered to safeguard his family. And that unknown is what reveals Imran Khan's exceptional courage. We have witnessed him enduring relentless persecution of his loved ones -false cases against his wife, Bushra Bibi, harassment of his sister and nephew. This persecution specifically targets his vulnerabilities, hoping to coerce compromise.

Yet we have seen nothing weaken Imran Khan's resolve. His conviction remains unwavering, his integrity uncompromised. Whatever the costs, he upholds the truth and fights for justice.

His family's immense suffering does not sway him from this righteous path.

This extraordinary steadfastness even in the face of persecution of his cherished ones sets Imran Khan apart. It is his profound faith, reinforced by "La ilaha illallah," that fortifies his spirit. He draws from the Divine strength to withstand any worldly pressure or pain.

My father protected us resolutely from smaller threats. But in the face of state oppression, only rare figures like Imran Khan demonstrate such ironclad courage and resilience. This supreme level of conviction and sacrifice for the greater good inspires awe. It is the mark of truly legendary leadership.

My father's ultimate sacrifice to protect us proves his singular devotion. Yet as a small individual, the full might of state oppression was untested for him. If my father had faced what Imran Khan endures --wilful campaigns against his family --could he have persevered? Would he have surrendered his beliefs to end their suffering? I cannot claim to know with certainty.

And that uncertainty in myself humbles me. For who among us can bear such torment of those we love most? When those dearest to our hearts are targeted, how many can endure it for a higher cause? The temptation to appease and compromise would be immense. But great leaders rise above such worldly foibles as attachment and fear. By surrendering completely to the Divine, they gather the strength to withstand any trial. Imran Khan stands apart in enduring the persecution of his wife, his sisters, his nephew. His profound faith reinforces an unbending conviction to remain righteous despite the persecution of his nearest and dearest.

This supreme resilience reveals true greatness. When Imran Khan sees his family tortured for his principles, his courage and dedication only grow firmer. This marks transcendent leadership capable of enormous sacrifice for the greater good. Few in history have matched such bravery in the face of intimate suffering.

My father died protecting his family, giving everything for those he loved. But Allah tests true messengers by persecuting those they love most. Remaining steadfast through such ultimate anguish separates the saintly from the rest of us. This exceptional conviction inspires awe at the power of sincere faith.

My late father stood apart in his community by fearlessly speaking truth and refusing to bow to those abusing power --be it influential people or even lowly officials playing god. For he recognised that respect stems not from worldly status but moral rectitude. Yet the society I come from has largely normalised the unIslamic practice of obeying the unjust, provided they hold power. Even within households, those who dare question unjust norms face derision. Corruption is rampant as the weak surrender to those who act above the law. This mentality infiltrates all levels. For instance, many excuse bending to the whims of even junior officials. A policeman demanding bribes is placated, not confronted. Out of either fear or indifference, few object even to daily injustice. Those who do protest such immoral subservience face accusations of being rude and disruptive. Their critics promote a warped idea of "respect" --accepting oppression to avoid confronting the oppressor. Speaking truth becomes "disrespect".

In this climate, the powerful freely manipulate religious rhetoric to perpetuate submission. Their tyranny is masked under the guise of maintaining social harmony. This is the insidious psychology of control dressed up as stability.

Rare voices like my father, who opposed this distorted status quo, were sidelined. But appeasing injustice only breeds criminality and inequality. This is the false peace of the graveyard, not tranquil coexistence.

Colonial rule may have formally ended but the mindset of

mental servility persists. Power, not principle, dictates norms. This is the legacy of induced inadequacy that convinces the subjugated their fate is fixed. But the Divine exhorts us to stand for justice, not acquiesce to wickedness. The Prophet upheld the meek, not the arrogant. True reformers therefore first transform the mindset that rationalises oppression. This jihad of the heart frees people from fear into moral courage.

My father walked this difficult road. He sacrificed comforts for contentment, safety for principle. This conviction guided him from self-interest to national interest. More embodying his example can yet liberate society from moral decay.

My father and Imran Khan have demonstrated an unwavering faith in "La ilaha illallah" that serves as my inspiration. Their lives' message is clear -upholding truth and justice demands tremendous courage and sacrifice. Yet I recognise within myself the need for much spiritual and moral training before reaching such stature. Their exemplary qualities did not arise overnight but were honed through lifelong struggle and surrender to the Divine.

Walking the path of integrity and purpose they have illuminated requires constantly overcoming the ego's worldly attachments and fears. I must strive daily to subjugate my own weaknesses to principles greater than myself. This jihad of the self is a lifelong challenge.

But their lives convince me the fruits of persevering are serenity and strength that surpass all earthly ambitions. My journey has only just begun, but their light guides the way forward. With humility, discipline and reliance on Allah, I hope to steadily nurture the moral courage their example demands.

Rarely is greatness thrust upon someone unprepared for its burdens. The path of righteousness necessitates patiently developing wisdom, fortitude and compassion to fulfil one's purpose. My father and leader attained spiritual perfection through enduring many trials. I, too, must earn through self-discipline what Allah wills for me. But the destination is worth any sacrifice.

Imam Hussain's unwavering stand at Karbala epitomised moral fortitude rooted in "La ilaha illallah" that endures adversity for truth and justice. His sacrifice lit an eternal flame of conviction that continues illuminating humanity across the ages.

The chain of devoted souls ready to sacrifice all for righteousness, which began with Prophets like Ibrahim and Isa, did not end with Imam Hussain. Through the centuries, the spirit of standing resolute against falsehood lived on in figures like Imam Ahmad bin Hanbal and Sultan Saladin Ayubi.

Imam Ahmad bin Hanbal (780–855 CE) was an influential Muslim scholar and theologian during the Abbasid Caliphate. He is considered the founder of the Hanbali school of Sunni Islamic jurisprudence (fiqh). Imam Ahmad bin Hanbal staunchly upheld orthodox religious beliefs based on the Qur'an and hadith, defending them against competing ideas and practices that compromised core tenets of Islam. He endured persecution and imprisonment for refusing to yield his positions under pressure from the Abbasid Caliph, becoming a revered figure for standing resolute against false ideologies.

Sultan Saladin Ayubi (1137–1193 CE) was the first sultan of Egypt and Syria during the 12th century. As a Muslim military and political leader, he led Islamic opposition, fighting against the Crusader states in the Levant and eventually recaptured Palestine. Known for his chivalry, he defeated European Crusaders at the decisive Battle of Hattin. His leadership and string of strategic victories made him a champion against the militaristic Crusades, which threatened Muslim control of sacred sites and inaccurate depictions of Islam. Revered as a heroic liberator and defender, his military campaigns opposed the religious falsehoods behind the Crusades.

Both figures thus exhibited steadfast resistance to false religious claims and were willing to suffer greatly for upholding truth. This made them inspirational models of resolutely standing against untruths through the ages. And thus, today, when oppression and sin appear triumphant, I see the embers of Imam Hussain's legacy stirring leaders like Imran Khan. Despite endless persecution, he upholds the truth with the same unwavering faith and resilience that defined Imam Hussain.

The names and faces change but the light remains the same, carried from era to era by devotees like Imran Khan. As it was for those before him, his path is that of speaking truth to power and striving for a just order, regardless of personal cost.

By Allah's decree, the chain of conscience embodied by Imam Hussain shall persist till the Day of Judgement. Whenever humanity plunges into moral decay, the Almighty raises reformers carrying the eternal flame that illuminates the righteous path again.

Imran Khan exemplifies courage and integrity rooted in profound faith in "La ilaha illallah," affirming that no deity but Allah warrants worship. His steadfast commitment to reform mirrors past leaders who revived Islam's just ethos against the justice.

Following the Prophets who confronted false beliefs, Imran Khan challenges modern kleptocracy and moral decay. His struggle embodies the Quranic call to fear no human, only the Divine. He remains undeterred by those peddling fear and coercion.

Persecution of Imran Khan's family has aimed to bend his resolve. But his spirit, strengthened by the Kalima, cannot be shaken. His audacity stems from this deep realisation no earthly shackles can enchain devotion to Allah and righteousness.

Upholding "La ilaha illallah," Imran Khan exemplifies

transformative leadership,-spurning personal gain to reform society based on Divine Will. His sustained commitment to fight injustice, despite virulent opposition, represents moral courage and farsightedness exceeding transient trials. By sparing nothing to advance the righteous order commanded by Allah, Imran Khan follows the path illuminated by Islam's greatest figures. His life reinforces that true strength comes from recognising Allah alone as sovereign authority and source of empowerment. May Imran Khan's sincerity keep brightening the path to justice. It's not just me who is thrilled by Khan's strong belief in "La ilaha." There are also millions of Khan's supporters who deeply admire his steadfast commitment to "La ilaha." Even respected legal experts on Khan's court team staunchly stand behind their client's firm conviction when it comes to his belief system and way of life. Clearly, appreciation for Khan's devoted creed runs far and wide, spanning all levels of advocacy in his defence.

Naeem Haider Panjutha, a promising young lawyer hailing from Sargodha, Pakistan, graduated with a law degree and immediately began practising law. Though he harboured ambitions of contesting the 2018 Pakistani elections, he ultimately did not end up running.

However, Panjutha found another outlet for his talents:-serving as a legal advocate for his long-time idol, Imran Khan. By his admission, Panjutha has been an ardent supporter of Khan for "countless reasons" over the years. He seized the opportunity to assist his hero when Khan took office as the prime minister of Pakistan, taking on his first power of attorney case on behalf of Khan while he was PM. Panjutha worked tirelessly day and night alongside his legal team on this landmark case, ultimately winning a victory for the prime minister. This first case centred around charges of defamation, though over time, Panjutha would assist Khan with an array of legal matters including other simple cases.

As Imran Khan took notice of the young lawyer's spirited efforts and successful track record, he rewarded Panjutha with increasing opportunities and responsibilities. Now, at the age of 33, Panjutha credits his rapid professional rise and fame - including high-profile interviews with renowned national and international media outlets -directly to the boost given by Imran Khan's support and patronage.

As Panjutha tells it: "Leaders like Khan give opportunities to youth. I'm just 33 and in this whatever fame I've as being interviewed by different renowned national and international media outlets, is all because of Imran Khan..." Expressing his profound gratitude, Panjutha remarked: "Imran Khan always supports youth and I'm one of such fortunate youths."

Currently, Naeem Haider Panjutha serves as one of Khan's personally approved lawyers granted visitation access to see him while he is jailed. After initially being barred from exercising, Panjutha reports that Khan is now provided a treadmill in his cell after the court intervened -allowing Khan to stay vigorous. According to Panjutha, Khan remains not only physically fit, but also in high spirits as he manoeuvres through this legal battle.

Naeem Haider Panjutha recently visited the incarcerated Imran Khan at Adyala Jail. He emerged astonished by the former prime minister's resolve, reporting: "Imran Khan is in much higher spirits and more determined than ever. His strength and resolution have multiplied manifold -as he now feels he has nothing to lose and has already won in the court of public opinion."

According to Panjutha, it is Khan who continues bolstering the morale and steeling the nerves of his band of lawyers. "We lawyers draw courage and passion from our leader Imran Khan. He inspires us that this is a war of nerves and we must stand resolute and fight through to the final ball," Panjutha revealed.

He depicted Khan as a stoic, almost heroic figure, who, paradoxically, wields more power behind bars than his rivals in government wield roaming free. "Khan is such a courageous man that even incarcerated, he remains the most powerful leader Pakistan has ever seen. His enemies may not be jailed, yet cower in fear of him -already tasting defeat," Panjutha reflected.

Beyond projecting strength, Imran Khan has also clearly delineated the central tenets of his legal battle for his lawyers to champion. As Panjutha tells it: "Khan is an exemplary leader - directing us lawyers to stay strong and reveal to the world how women suffer in Pakistan without rights, how the constitution lies dissolved, and lawlessness prevails."

With Khan's guidance fuelling their advocacy, Panjutha and his colleagues have shed light on issues from human rights violations to the erosion of democratic norms to the breakdown of civil society under the current regime.

Along with the rest of Imran Khan's legal team, Naeem Haider Panjutha has increasingly faced grave threats from the state for his representation of the ousted prime minister. He discloses that he has received sinister warnings through close associates from Khan's political enemies seeking to intimidate him.

As one of Khan's lead lawyers, Panjutha had a front-row view of the chaotic scene on 9 May 2023 when Khan was illegally detained by Rangers forces right inside the courtroom premises. As over 100 armed Rangers officers and police forcibly surrounded Khan, Panjutha desperately tried to intervene,-recognising the outright illegality of Khan's arrest unfolding before his eyes.

"I refused to stand by while this miscarriage of justice happened and instead tried to protect my client. But I was attacked and left bleeding from gashes on my head and nose that likely required stitches," Panjutha revealed. However, despite his injuries, the young lawyer refused to go to the hospital and instead remained stationed at the court complex until nearly midnight -tirelessly exploring every possible legal avenue to free Khan from unjust imprisonment.

What compels this 33-year-old advocate to show such fearlessness and devotion defending Imran Khan, even at great personal cost? According to Panjutha, Khan is the only national leader he has witnessed willing to sacrifice his own safety to fight for Pakistan's future. Moreover, Panjutha stresses that over his extensive political career, Khan has consistently maintained his honesty -untouched by the corruption allegations that taint most officials.

Yet for all his massive popularity, Khan retains a level of personal humility rarely seen from such an iconic public figure. Panjutha fondly recalls: "During court proceedings, Khan himself would stand and approach us lawyers to discuss developments and strategy. Unlike most influential elites in Pakistan who summon their lawyers to them, Khan always showed us the highest respect."

In Panjutha's perspective, Imran Khan's exceptional blend of courageous leadership, incorruptible integrity, and modest character makes him a national hero worth suffering for. These extraordinary qualities explain the intense loyalty Khan inspires in promising young advocates like Naeem Haider Panjutha.

The threats facing Naeem Haider Panjutha have now escalated from chilling warnings to concrete legal action meant to intimidate him. As Panjutha reveals: "There are multiple FIRs registered against me, compelling me to go into hiding and even abandon my own home."

Yet Imran Khan's lead counsel remains undeterred, recently taking up temporary residence in Khan's Bani Gala estate to continue coordinating his legal strategy out of harm's way. As Panjutha defiantly declares: "Nothing can stop me from standing shoulder-to-shoulder with my leader in his fight for justice. My love and loyalty to Imran Khan overcome all fear."

Beyond inspiring bravery, working closely alongside Khan has imprinted Naeem Panjutha with life-shaping wisdom. He specifies two prime mantras he has internalised from his mentor: "Firstly, never give up on seemingly impossible goals, as struggle can achieve anything. Secondly, persist daily in inch-by-inch progress towards your defined mission."

Most profoundly, Panjutha credits Khan with cementing his faith in the Divine, recounting: "I have learnt to truly believe in La Ilaha (There is no God but Allah) due to Imran Khan's influence."

This grounding in courage, perseverance and spirituality steels Panjutha's resolve to stand by Khan's side though any storms ahead. As he proclaims: "I will always support Imran Khan's legal fight no matter the costs, because he represents the leader I have chosen to follow into the future."

Steadfast against all looming troubles, Naeem Haider Panjutha has indelibly hitched his fortunes to Imran Khan's star -prepared to endure immense personal sacrifices to advance his leader's vision for national revival. This loyalty testifies to the Moldovan calibre of advocates Khan attracts even in his moment of tribulation.

2

"IYYAKA NA'BUDU WA IYYAKA NASTA'EEN"

TURNING TO ALLAH IN PRAYER AND WORSHIP

إِيَّاكَ نَعْبُدُ وَإِيَّاكَ نَسْتَعِينِ The phrase "Iyyaka Na'budu wa Iyyaka Nasta'een" is the opening of Surah Al-Fatiha, the first chapter of the Quran. It translates to "It is You we worship and You we ask for help." This verse establishes the relationship between God and human beings in Islam.

Some key points about this verse:

It affirms that worship is directed solely to God. Muslims submit to and worship Allah alone, not any other beings, idols or entities.

It highlights that God is the sole source of help and refuge. Muslims rely on and seek assistance from Allah for all their needs.

The use of "You" and "we" indicates a direct connection between worshipper and God.

The verse sets the tone for the rest of the Quran -the message that surrender, worship and seeking help are directed to Allah alone.

It encapsulates the essence of Islam --affirming the Oneness of God, following His commandments and seeking His aid. This verse is recited in every unit of Islamic prayer.

So in summary, this opening verse of Surah Al-Fatiha establishes the devotion and servitude of human beings to Allah, which is a fundamental concept in Islam. The entire Quran elaborates on the relationship dynamics embedded in this verse.

My leader, Imran Khan, the former prime minister of Pakistan, and chairman of the Pakistan Tehreek-e-Insaf (PTI) party, has frequently invoked the Quranic verse "Iyyaka Na'budu wa Iyyaka Nasta'een" (You alone we worship, and You alone we ask for help) in his political speeches and public addresses over the years.

This verse from Surah Al-Fatiha, the opening chapter of the Holy Quran, succinctly encapsulates the essence of the relationship between God and human beings in Islam --one defined by devotion, submission, and reliance solely upon the Almighty. By initiating his speeches with this verse, Imran Khan indicates that his political vision and life mission are firmly grounded in Islamic teachings.

While this short Quranic phrase is not technically a verse from Khan himself, its recurrent use underscores his deep personal piety and identity as a Muslim. By referring to it so often, he implicitly reminds his audiences and followers that his journey as a cricketer-turned-politician has been guided by faith above all else.

Ever since entering politics in the mid-1990s with the aim of building a "Naya Pakistan,"Khan has underscored his religious motivation. His very first political speech delivered at Lahore in 1997 began with recitation of Surah Al-Fatiha and introduction of the "Iyyaka Na'budu wa Iyyaka Nasta'een" verse -a practice he would continue for decades. Whether addressing college students, world leaders, diaspora crowds or his own party workers, Khan has made it a point to invoke the Quran before diving into his political vision.

For instance, in a 2013 rally, months before PTI's rise as a major political force, he repeated this verse, stressing that he seeks Allah's help alone in his campaign for justice and anti-corruption reforms. Similarly, his 2018 election speech commenced with this verse, as he framed his push for Naya Pakistan as being guided by Islamic ideals of honesty, humanity and accountability.

Even as prime minister delivering his last speech in April 2022 before being ousted via a vote of no-confidence, he recited Surah Al-Fatiha and emphasised "Iyyaka Na'budu wa Iyyaka Nasta'een" --reaffirming his conviction that his struggle represents far more than politics and is deeply rooted in spiritual foundations.

Beyond just introducing speeches, Khan makes frequent references to this Quranic phrase in interviews and media engagements as well. He often points out how it underpins his refusal to compromise with corrupt forces, since he bows only to Allah, not worldly power brokers. Whenever questioned about the basis of his bold political positions and perseverance, he alludes to this verse, highlighting his commitment to principle and higher moral purpose.

Overall, Imran Khan's consistent invocation of "Iyyaka Na'budu wa Iyyaka Nasta'een" over a 25-years-plus political career reveals much about his personality and leadership style. It shows he derives strength from his Muslim identity and faith, which provide him moral courage to take strong stances regardless of opposition. It points to his unwavering belief that with trust in God, the people of Pakistan can achieve justice and national rejuvenation.

And with his unrelenting repetition of this Quranic phrase, he has promoted Islamic values like truth, integrity and reform to wider audiences. In fact, many of his supporters themselves now initiate public events or political rallies by reciting Surah Al-Fatiha and echoing "Iyyaka Na'budu wa Iyyaka Nasta'een" --reminding all that Khan's vision reflects desire for a state and system guided by Quranic ideals of righteousness.

So while just seven words in length, this profoundly resonant verse from Surah Al-Fatiha has become deeply intertwined with Imran Khan's political image and worldview. Its regular invocation in his oratory sheds light on the sincerity of his faith-based motivations. And the widespread uptake of this phrase by his followers reflects Khan's success in pairing Islamic ethics with political advocacy. Overall, "Iyyaka Na'budu wa Iyyaka Nasta'een" succinctly captures the essence of Khan's spiritual-political outlook.

While materialism and unjust power structures have corroded Pakistani society, it would be unwise to assume spiritual bankruptcy among the people. Many still lead lives of faith, ethics and community uplift, per the essence of "Iyyaka Na'budu wa Iyyaka Nasta'een."

No doubt, the elite capture of resources and suppression of marginalised groups has bred inequality and discontent. However, neighbours still support each other, Islamic charity thrives, and belief in Allah's sovereignty remains strong among the underprivileged. Sincere Pakistanis engage in efforts big and small to lift society.

Mainstream religious voices regularly speak out against division and for harmony. Spiritual messages of unity resonate widely even if fringe elements grab headlines. Underdevelopment in provinces like Balochistan and KP understandably fuels separatism. Yet countless civilians raise these issues through legal and ethical means, guided by Quranic principles.

Moreover, Imran Khan's decades-long political struggle has inspired many Pakistani youths and common people to renew their commitment to the deeper message behind "Iyyaka Na'budu." His vision, grounded in faith, justice and selflessness has awakened a higher moral consciousness regarding duty to society and has led to greater political engagement.

While Pakistan faces socio-economic and governance deficits, the essence of Surah Fatiha continues to drive personal spirituality and public service efforts. Cynicism about people's values risks being unfair. The Quranic ideal represented in "Iyyaka Na'budu" endures in the daily manifestations of faith, compassion and justice exhibited by countless Pakistanis. Khan's movement has revived its true spirit, fuelling hope for reform guided by moral purpose.

Imran Khan's decades-long struggle against corruption and for justice has resonated across ethnicities, including among Pashtuns like the courageous leaders Murad Saeed, Ali Muhammad Khan, Shehryar Afridi and his lawyer Sher Afzal Marwat. His perseverance despite opposition, his grounding in strong values, and his ability to awaken higher purpose in disillusioned citizens, especially youth, earns widespread respect. Khan's open reliance on faith connects to citizens who share such beliefs and seek a more principled society. His wider message rejuvenates hope in Pakistan's future as per its founding vision. For many, Khan represents authentic leadership towards realising Quranic ideals like "Iyyaka Na'budu" through both conviction and action. While avoiding assumptions about individuals' private views, Khan's public conduct motivates citizens towards reform and re-commitment to moral purpose.

I'm certain that my father smiles from heavens seeing me choosing my leader Imran Khan and standing by him. I couldn't make him more proud with my choice of leader.

During Imran Khan's judicial remand in jail, he has requested several books, including the Quran and other Islamic texts, as well as works on history, politics, and spirituality. This suggests Khan aims to continue his self-improvement and intellectual curiosity even in difficult circumstances. His interest in spiritual texts affirms his frequently stated grounding in faith and moral principles.

Here's the list of books he is going to read during the period:

How Democracies Die by Steven Levitsky & Daniel Ziblatt

Monsoon by Robert D. Kaplan

A People's History of the United States by Howard Zinn

Guns, Germs, and Steel by Jared Diamond

World Order by Henry Kissinger

Secrets of Divine Love

The Narrow Corridor

Active Measures

The Revenge of Geography

Indus Divided

Empires of the Indus

The China-Pakistan Axis

Balthasar's Odyssey

The Next 100 Years

As Through a Veil

A Drift

The reading of such books aligns with Khan's frequent references to the importance of moral purpose and continuous self-improvement as a leader.

Throughout his public life, Imran Khan has cultivated an image as a leader guided by strong moral purpose. As a cricket-star-turned-politician, his speeches often emphasise the importance of integrity, justice, and national sovereignty for leaders to make a positive impact.

Khan frequently cites philosophical and spiritual works as influencing his uncompromising principles. For example, he has recommended books like Plato's Republic, and the Sufi poet Rumi as essential reading for those who wish to develop wisdom. Khan sees self-reflection and personal growth as critical for leaders to serve their people justly.

This focus on moral development aligns with Khan's own trajectory from sportsman to political stalwart over decades. His supporters, including me, see his refusal to compromise despite obstacles as flowing from deep personal conviction. To me and his other admirers, Khan's stubborn adherence to his values in the face of opposition represents inspirational strength.

Umar Niaz Khan, 40, PTI Youth Coordinator in Abu Dhabi since 2017, recalls being enthralled by Imran Khan's mass appeal since 2008 within his native Pashtun community in the rural Bannu region along the Pakistan-Afghanistan borderlands. For him and his fellow villagers, no other modern figure or party compares after experiencing Khan's grassroots engagement uplifting marginalised border populations long exploited by central authorities.

He recounts: "We Pashtuns have always stood by Khan and willingly sacrifice everything for him because he comprehends the essence of our alienation and fights for identity, rights and resources long denied." Other opportunist leaders and parties promising change came and went from their remote villages, but only Khan walked the talk over the decades, be it championing Pashtun welfare or building the world-class Shaukat Khanum cancer hospital, where penniless patients receive cutting-edge care for free.

Niaz Khan underwent lifesaving surgery there for a kidney tumour during Khan's tenure as prime minister, experiencing first-hand humanitarian policies benefiting everyday citizens irrespective of privilege, ethnicity or creed - core to the Pashtunwali code of honour and human dignity. It cemented his gratitude and loyalty as he recovered to full health without bearing any financial burden. He queries rhetorically: "Could any other leader or party ever uplift my people so comprehensively through words and deeds?"

For him, the current regime's ouster of Khan's legitimate

government smacks of old conspiracies by powerful institutions to subvert leaders daring to confront defence-heavy status quos short-changing Pashtuns. "Our blood boils witnessing peaceful protestors, especially educated progressive youth, jailed under sedition charges. But nothing can deter us from this freedom struggle after tasting rights and self-respect under an administration that defended our interests."

Now coordinating global diaspora resistance through his fiery Twitter forum, attracting supporters and allies from all spheres, Niaz declares uncompromising moral support for his jailed leader. "What Ghaffar Khan and Bacha Khan started cannot be crushed now. Our loyalties, tested over generations of oppression, will fuel this non-violent civil disobedience. Khan awakened us to contest elections as mechanism for change. Authority's worst excesses only strengthen our resolve. We will bring this illegitimate dictatorship down, come what may!"

Umar Niaz Khan credits Imran Khan with reawakening within Pashtuns the profound meaning behind the Islamic attestation of faith -"Iyyaka Na'budu Wa Iyyaka Nasta'een". He expands on how Khan embodies this divine connection that has inspired tribal groups feeling abandoned by prevailing political forces for generations.

The defiant proclamation affirms unwavering loyalty towards no sovereign except the Creator who ordains moral order upon humanity. By upholding truth and justice above fleeting mortal kings obsessed with temporal power, the oppressed draw indomitable strength. For Khan does not manipulate faith to secure votes but calls for inner reformation towards accountability and equity as the highest manifestation of worshipping Allah.

It contrasts stark politicians campaigning from mosque pulpits but betraying voters as soon as elections conclude. Their forked tongues alternately palliate the public with piety or militancy for votes according to cynical opportunity. Khan urges transcending such manipulation by walking a righteous path - even solo if the situation demands - as a true marker of spiritual mettle, rather than chasing crowds down roads of hypocrisy. Standing upright for ethical principles earns divine assistance where numbers or equipment prove inadequate.

Through selfless commitment over decades towards humanitarian causes benefiting the downtrodden, irrespective of identity markers, Khan awakens that covenant binding humanity to collective welfare as duty onto the Divine. Where his predecessors and rivals rule by division and distraction, Khan insists on reimagining national purpose rooted in advancing social justice and prosperity cooperatively. This rejects marginalising or scapegoating vulnerable groups for political expedience which has triggered economic ruination and militant radicalisation in cycles. Upholding the dignity of even the weakest citizen opens blessings exceeding worldly calculations.

Thus, Pashtun groups find Khan uniquely understanding their long trauma, and being willing to redress inequities fuelling conflict. His consistent advocacy against the brutal bombing of tribal villages, guided by conscientious restraint, contrasts with his predecessors itching to prove military prowess even at the expense of innocent blood. Seeking restorative healing and addressing root causes earns him respect from besieged communities long demonised by the media or exploited callously by authorities from afar. They discern sincerity beyond political pretenders who have never sacrificed privilege or comfort.

For Khan extends the true Islamic teaching of godliness manifesting in selfless service towards creating a just, inclusive and progressive society, aligning divine commands with enlightened statecraft. Defending such vision against usurpers draws spontaneous mobilisation from youth, women, and workers feeling agents of historical resistance against both oppression and apathy...rejecting status quos failing their spiritual calling. Reclaiming destiny as their sole rightful worship and seeking divine assistance for justice flows naturally when corrupt orders decay moral purpose. By modelling that world, transcending commitment to principle whatever the temporal cost, Khan awakens the lion spirit latent within Pashtun conscience.

3

"COMPROMISE FOR YOUR DREAM BUT NEVER COMPROMISE ON YOUR DREAM"

FOLLOWING YOUR VISION

Ambition is a fundamental human trait that drives us to aspire towards goals and dreams. However, left unchecked, ambition can also lead some down an unethical path in the relentless pursuit of success. A nuanced understanding of ambition is required.

From an early age, ambition starts manifesting as simple dreams -a child wishing to get a new toy or learn a new skill. These small dreams push the child to take steps out of their comfort zone and learn. But sometimes parental pressure can impose unrealistic expectations, overriding the child's own desires.

As we grow older, ambition shapes our career and life visions. Some, like scientists, may hold ambitious dreams to make path-breaking discoveries. Entrepreneurs aspire to build innovative companies. Songwriters and artists harbour ambitions to touch people's lives creatively. But ambition without integrity can result in unethical business practices, plagiarism, greed and exploitation in these fields.

Ambition need not be only for material success. Those committed to social justice dedicate their lives towards ambitious visions of a more equal world. Non-profit workers ambition big projects to serve communities. But even seemingly altruistic ambitions can be corrupted by a desire for power over others.

Ultimately, ambition must be guided by a moral compass and wisdom. Well-directed ambition aligned with one's values can achieve great things. But unchecked ambition tangent to ethics and humanity inevitably leads to problems at both personal and societal levels. By cultivating mindful self-awareness, we can harness ambition as a force for good.

The key is recognising that ambition itself is ethically neutral - neither good nor bad intrinsically. Only by embedding it within a framework of compassion, moderation and integrity can ambition enable individuals to realise their highest potential as human beings. An enlightened society nurtures ambition, while restraining its excesses. However, ambition is most effective when driven by a principled vision, rather than unchecked ambition that can lead to compromise and danger.

In Shakespeare's tragedy, Macbeth, unbridled ambition devoid of a moral compass leads the protagonist towards tyranny and ruin. Blindly ambitious and urged on by prophecy, Macbeth pursues the crown through murder and betrayal, only to cause his own downfall.

In contrast, many of history's greatest reformers demonstrated ambition firmly grounded in ethical vision. Mahatma Gandhi ambitiously led nationwide non-violent resistance to liberate India from British rule. His ambitious vision was guided by the principled aim of securing freedom through non-violence. Martin Luther King Jr. ambitiously spearheaded the civil rights movement, inspired by his Christian vision of racial equality and justice.

Similarly, Nelson Mandela ambitiously fought apartheid in South Africa based on the morally ambitious goal of establishing a multi-racial democracy with equal rights for all. In all these cases, high ambition served an enlightened ideal rather than personal advancement. This gave their efforts deep resonance.

Qaid-e-Azam Jinnah ambitiously led the struggle for an independent homeland for Muslims amidst high tensions and uncertainty. Despite his initially moderate political leanings, Jinnah's vision was shaped by his principled aim of securing the Muslim community's democratic rights and freedom from discrimination. His ethical ambition united disparate groups behind a common cause.

Fatima Jinnah demonstrated equal ambition by championing her brother's vision. She campaigned tirelessly for Pakistan's creation, and later for civil liberties against military rule. Her support was ambitious yet rooted in integrity rather than personal fame.

Abdul Sattar Edhi's life mission was the ambitious vision of building Pakistan's largest volunteer ambulance network dedicated entirely to social welfare. He devoted himself to this principled cause despite limited means, motivated by selfless ambition to aid the marginalised. His family shared this ambition for purpose-driven service.

Finally, Imran Khan ambitiously pursued political change inspired by the principled vision of creating a corruption-free, socially just Pakistan. Criticised for lacking political experience, he persevered over decades guided by this ambitious yet ethical vision for reform, not power. While their specific contexts differed, these leaders displayed ambition propelled by moral purpose and vision for uplifting their communities, their eyes fixed firmly on ethical goals rather than personal glory or enrichment. This marriage of ambition to principle allowed them to gain wide respect and leave enduring legacies.

Of course, ambition unchecked by ethics can lead even

well-intentioned leaders down dangerous paths, as seen in Stalin's tyrannical decades-long rule over the Soviet Union after the Russian revolution. A prudent balance is required.

Shortly, ambition united to a vision greater than oneself often achieves what unprincipled ambition cannot. A modest spirit seeking to serve a principled cause taps into human aspirations for meaning. Ambition with moral foundations can elevate, rather than corrupt societies. With ethical ambition, ordinary individuals too can achieve extraordinary things.

For decades, corruption by political elites was an open secret in Pakistan but rarely confronted directly. Much of the public became desensitised to revelations of financial misdeeds and conflicts of interest among their leaders. This systemic corruption seemed immutable. Imran Khan shattered this resignation by making accountability and reform the centrepiece of his politics. His relentless emphasis on corruption as the root of Pakistan's problems helped turn it into a mainstream electoral issue. By regularly highlighting instances of elite capture, graft and self-dealing, Khan kept the spotlight fixed on corruption that people had become numb to. His uncompromising stand forced even political opponents to pay lip-service to ending corruption.

Mainstream discourse shifted as Khan framed corruption not just as financial but moral decay. His mass rallies resonated with people fed up of dishonesty in public life. He tapped into an undercurrent of unease, converting it into a national anti-corruption consciousness. Years of Khan's persistent messaging and awareness-raising helped strip away the veneer from questionable practices that had become normalised and invisible. Brazen conflicts of interest now faced public scrutiny.

Of course, eradicating systemic graft will take sustained structural and behavioural change. However, Imran Khan's greatest achievement has been stimulating transparency and accountability into becoming defining election issues. He compelled the public to confront corruption that had become endemic but accepted. This demonstration of principled politics challenging entrenched power has raised the standards of what citizens expect from leadership. There is now an awakened culture of questioning rather than acquiescence to dishonesty in office. Imran Khan's struggle primed people to be less tolerant of unethical conduct by public representatives.

While Pakistan has a long way to go in actualising reform, Khan's tireless campaign has been instrumental in creating an anti-corruption ethos and expectations for integrity. By resolutely making corruption the defining fight of his politics, he mainstreamed a critical national conversation.

Visionary leaders are often pioneers who chart new courses rather than follow well-worn paths. They dream ambitiously of changing entrenched systems and norms for the betterment of society. This requires them to take the road less travelled - full of uncertainty and opposition, but aligned with their values and vision. Their ambition is fuelled by the imagination to create what does not yet exist.

For example, Nelson Mandela faced severe backlash for advocating armed resistance against apartheid. Yet his ambitiously principled vision of a democratic multiracial South Africa kept him undeterred through decades of prison. Today, he is hailed worldwide as a pioneer.

Similarly, Martin Luther King Jr. braved vitriol and violence to pave America's road to racial justice. Rosa Parks defiantly sat in a whites-only bus seat, powering the Montgomery bus boycott that accelerated the fight for equal rights.

In India, Jawaharlal Nehru daringly navigated the untested path towards an independent, democratic state despite the odds stacked against this vision. The ambitious dreams of such trailblazers were powered by farsighted vision and values, not personal glory.

This willingness to undertake difficult, uncharted roads for the sake of a principled vision is what marks out transformative leaders. By imagining alternative realities aligned with justice, they turn ambition into action and pave new trails for societies to follow.

Of course, realising ambitious dreams requires collaborating with those inspired by the vision. But history remembers pioneering leaders who embarked first down difficult roads towards progress. Their principled ambition and imagination lights the way forward for others.

In his novel, The Alchemist, Paulo Coelho wrote the now famous line: "When you want something, all the universe conspires in helping you to achieve it." This expresses a belief that when you focus your intentions on a dream, forces seem to align mysteriously to assist you. While some dismiss this as wishful thinking, the concept resonates with the "law of attraction" theorised in self-help and spiritual philosophies. This law states that concentrating mentally on goals and believing in their realisation attracts people, resources and events to aid accomplishment.

However, critics argue this oversimplifies achievement by ignoring systemic obstacles and privilege differences. Positive thinking alone cannot guarantee success. Hard work, skill development and seizing opportunities matter greatly. At the same time, research does show the power of visualisation, positive expectations and mental framing in achievement to some extent. Placebo effects demonstrate that beliefs shape reality. So mindset does play a role in manifesting dreams, though likely not as decisively as some claim.

In practice, sensible balance is required. Dreams do need active effort, not just passive "attraction" of desired results. But cultivating optimism and mental focus can become self-fulfilling prophecies. We may naturally notice and capitalise on opportunities more when positively oriented towards a vision.

Overall, while deeper forces are at play, believing in one's dreams passionately can generate the motivation, tenacity and openness needed to achieve ambitious goals. Coelho's quote contains some truth - with the caveat that dreams require proactive work to fulfill, not just vision boards and positive vibes. Strategic effort aligned to purposeful ambition is key.

In short, the mindset of harnessing the universe's support for one's dreams, as Coelho suggests, resonates when combined with diligent, thoughtful action toward clearly defined goals. Internal clarity and conviction do subtly influence external realities to assist the manifestation of dreams. But sole reliance on cosmic attraction is unrealistic.

Leaders like Imran Khan do demonstrate the powerful effects of maintaining positivity and hopeful determination even in the face of challenges. His decades-long struggle exhibits admirable perseverance fuelled by retaining a constructive mindset and orientation towards his vision for reform.

Imran Khan often references impactful quotes and ideas in his public speeches, including the famous line by Maulana Rumi: "If God has given you strength to fly, why creep?" This rhetorical question conveys the message that we should aspire to reach our greatest potential.

Maulana Rumi was a highly influential 13th-century Persian poet, Islamic scholar, and Sufi mystic considered one of the greatest figures in Islamic literary culture. His revered epics, Masnavi and Diwan-e Shams-e Tabrizi, are among the masterpieces of mystical Sufi poetry. Rumi's teachings emphasise seeking the inner spiritual meaning of life.

The quote "If God has given you strength to fly, why creep?" is drawn from a famous story in Rumi's Masnavi. It uses the metaphor of a snake advised to stop slithering on the ground and instead rise up to discover its hidden abilities. This expresses encouragement to shed perceived limitations, nurture ambitious dreams, and fulfill one's highest potential rather than resigning to mediocrity. When Imran Khan invokes this quote, he taps into Rumi's inspirational message to motivate people to dream big and diligently work to uplift themselves and society. The quote resonates strongly with Khan's calls - especially to youth - to reject negativity and cynicism, discover their talents, and actively participate in reforming the nation. By citing one of Islamic history's most spiritually influential mystical figures, Khan amplifies his own message of ambition, self-empowerment and social justice. His use of Rumi draws upon generations of cultural reverence for the poet's teachings to reinforce Khan's reformist vision of societal change driven by the people reaching their full potential.

In a nutshell, this impactful quote by Maulana Rumi expresses an empowering sentiment that connects effectively with Imran Khan's political messaging aimed at energizing the populace for positive change.

It makes sense why so many people connect with Khan's gutsy goals and real talk about issues. Leaders who get folks fired up usually have a way with words and can tie big ideas together with hopes and dreams that we all have. Khan seems to have that way. He can lay out a big goal, like ending poverty, in a way that feels within reach - like he has thought hard about all the steps needed to get there. And he explains things without getting all high and mighty or talking over people's heads. So while those ambitious, thoughtful ideas might be what first captures people's attention, it's likely his down-to-earth communication style that helps those messages stick and makes people want to follow him. You can just tell he cares and gets what everyday folks care about too. A pretty powerful combo for a leader - thinking big and talking straight. I can see why that makes him inspiring to many.

It's also understandable why Imran Khan's public persona

and stated principles resonate with many people, such as his calls for transparency, reform, and uplifting humanity. His bold vision and determination have struck a chord, especially among youth. Supporters are attracted to qualities they associate with him, like truthfulness and consistency. However, it is important not to place any leader on a pedestal or make sweeping claims that the entire populace admires them. There are citizens with reasons for criticising or opposing Khan based on different political alignments, values or policy priorities. For instance, some criticise centralised governance, question his managerial expertise or dispute his stance on certain issues.

In a democratic dispensation, followership must be built on rational assessment of leaders' actions, not just stated values. Even those we align strongly with should be engaged with intellectually. Blind loyalty devoid of accountability risks worse outcomes than reasonable disagreement.

Based on the valid reasons of visionary leadership skills, many, especially youth, feel represented by Khan's reformist zeal. And his rise does indicate deep desire for change from the status quo. However, balance requires conceding that thoughtful opposition also exists for some reasons.

After being ousted as prime minister of Pakistan, Imran Khan has frequently invoked the names Mir Jafar and Mir Sadiq in his public speeches. By referring to these infamous historical figures known for betraying their rulers, Khan accuses certain contemporary politicians of treachery and compromising national interests.

Mir Jafar was a military commander in 18th-century Bengal, under the region's Nawab, Siraj ud-Daulah. He betrayed Siraj and conspired with the British East India Company during the pivotal Battle of Plassey in 1757. This treason allowed the British to defeat Siraj, and paved the way for the British Empire to colonize Bengal. "Mir Jafar" became a term for traitors willing to collude with colonial powers against national interests.

Similarly, in late 18th-century Mysore, minister Mir Sadiq covertly allied with the British against his own ruler Tipu Sultan, leaking state secrets that enabled British forces to infiltrate and defeat Mysore. "Mir Sadiq" also became an epithet for those who betray their country or ruler for personal power and wealth.

When modern politicians are labeled "Mir Jafar" or "Mir Sadiq" by figures like Imran Khan, it invokes these historical betrayals to accuse them of compromising national interests through collusion with foreign powers like the United States.

It is true that even within Imran Khan's own party, there have been cases of perceived betrayal by certain members who "stabbed from the back," as we've seen. At the same time, Khan does appear to have some genuinely devoted allies and workers as well, by his account. Realistically, all leaders will make mistakes in trusting certain individuals; complete infallibility cannot be expected. Khan himself acknowledges errors in judgement, like perhaps relying overly on the assurances of figures like ex-army chief General Qamar Bajwa.

Yet, admitting mistakes is a sign of responsible leadership. Historic leaders have acknowledged missteps too. As humans, none of us are immune to occasional errors, regardless of stature.

While Khan's core supporters understandably idealise him, it is healthy to maintain the perspective that even well-intentioned leaders can make poor decisions. Measured analysis should not overlook both accomplishments and misjudgements. Blind hero-worship devoid of respectful critique risks poor outcomes.

George Washington, despite enormous successes as America's first president, acknowledged making strategic missteps early in the Revolutionary War that resulted in losing battles to the British. He demonstrated accountable leadership by adapting his tactics based on analysing those initial failures.

Abraham Lincoln is considered one of the greatest presidents ever, but he openly admitted appointing inexperienced generals early in the Civil War, which led to stinging defeats for the Union army. Lincoln took responsibility for these judgement errors and learned from them. Winston Churchill was one of Britain's most celebrated prime ministers. Yet he too conceded underestimating Japanese naval power at the outset of World War II, contributing to costly British losses. Churchill recognised these failures honestly in order to adjust strategy appropriately.

Even hugely revered reformist leaders like Nelson Mandela admitted committing violent acts of resistance initially before realising only non-violence could effectively end apartheid. Mandela exemplified responsible leadership by acknowledging past mistakes in his journey.

While successes ultimately define great leaders, those who candidly own major missteps when warranted earn respect for accountability. Even the most accomplished figures in history made impactful errors, but learned from transparently admitting them rather than hiding flaws.

The hallmark of an ethical a leader as Khan is a willingness to transparently acknowledge major errors in judgement when proven through facts, and clarify how they intend to learn from those missteps going forward. Although a well-respected figure, Khan has mostly been open to valid criticism and feedback. Hubris and inflexibility in never conceding faults, regardless of evidence, risks poor decision-making. On the other hand, addressing shortcomings objectively, without defensiveness, garners public trust and helps leaders improve, as evidenced by in Khan's case.

I remember that a few days before his passing, my father had a harsh exchange of words with one of our tenants. Initially he remained frustrated about the argument. However, my father's sense of ethics compelled him to take the mature step of approaching the tenant to apologize sincerely for his role. Though a simple act, my father's humility in that moment left an indelible mark on me. It embodied the courage and strength of character required for anyone in a leadership role - whether of a family or an entire nation -to self-reflect, admit mistakes, and make amends through apology.

True leaders distinguish themselves not by stubbornly clinging to ego or a sense of perfection, but by recognising their humanity. My father's principled example shaped my firm belief that the greatest figures are those who retain the modesty to correct themselves when required, regardless of their stature. His act of making peace demonstrated the subduing of ego that elevates one's nobility.

The memory of my father's dignified apology, though a small personal incident, crystallized for me the essence of enlightened leadership. It takes moral strength to conquer one's pride, make peace, and earn respect by doing what is right, not what is ego-satisfying. I am grateful to have had such virtuous role models in my life.

Hearing my chosen leader openly admit past mistakes and express a willingness to learn from them fills me with appreciation for his integrity. Unfortunately, the powerful military establishment and political players in Pakistan rarely acknowledge major missteps transparently. For instance, the grievous mistakes that led to the secession of East Pakistan took place decades ago, yet remain unaccounted for through public truth and reconciliation.

While ordinary citizens have healed, establishing the principle of accountability could help regain lost trust. We see instead that the lack of transparent self-appraisal allows core systemic issues to persist, rather than be addressed decisively. Confessing errors requires courage, but can unlock forgiveness and unity.

Leaders who humbly invite objective feedback signal

strength, not weakness. By inspiring culture change from the top, they enable institutions to acknowledge uncomfortable truths, learn collaboratively, and thus evolve constructively. My leader's frankness gives me hope that transparent self-appraisal could become the norm, helping establish ethics-bound governance. The people are inclined to applaud leaders who demonstrate moral courage in admitting missteps sincerely and focusing on redressal. While compromise for national interest is prudent, true progress requires embracing accountability.

Shab Niaz Khan, 35, Central Executive Member of PTI's Insaf Youth Federation, relates his harrowing ordeal facing anti-terrorism charges for participation in peaceful protests after the false flag of 9 May 2023. As senior KP Province youth leader, multiple FIRs accused him of sedition despite having no evidence, shocking his family.

However, the brutal crackdown proved a watershed moment, awakening Pakistani conscience to the corrupt system's realities. Niaz Khan explains: "Through terror charges against me and thousands of other innocent dissidents, the regime's brazen weaponisation of law enforcement machinery against ordinary citizens itself gave the nation a stark glimpse into coercive state machinery operating without accountability."

He continues: "The coordinated demonisation, illegal abductions, denial of fundamental rights and a type of compromised judiciary reminded people why Imran Khan devoted over two decades to struggling against such an entrenched repressive status quo lacking any legitimacy." System defects, once easy to ignore when targeting nameless statistics in peripheries, now affected educated urban households, unexpectedly catalysing solidarity across classes.

And the resistance movement protecting fundamental constitutional liberties continues gaining strength each day, our leader Imran Khan framed in one false case after another the closer he gets to reaching Islamabad. Khan's refusal to compromise under threats or pressure gives followers the courage to absorb regime persecution without surrendering. Niaz avows: "The fight goes on until total system change. Too late for piecemeal reform -this freedom struggle aims to permanently emancipate all institutions from dynastic political interference, ensuring rule of law and justice."

With defiant chants of "Imported Government Na Manzoor" reverberating nationwide from swelling crowds courting arrests alongside Khan, Niaz discerns the corrupt regime's days are numbered. "The passionate fervour for 'Haqeeqi Azadi' has already seized national imagination, soon to sweep away colluders selling out sovereignty. No weaponry can extinguish the flame of an awakened citizenry's thirst for reclaiming birth right to dignified existence under accountable democratic governance. Khan ignited this unstoppable revolution. The nation stands ready to make all necessary sacrifices until we taste freedom."

Shab Niaz Khan relates how shocking scenes of police brutality against Imran Khan and his legal team during a court appearance on 9 May outraged entire households, including women rarely active politically. He explains: "Footage of our revered leader dragged violently from court premises energised not just youth but mothers and sisters in my village who now actively encourage us upholding the right to peaceful dissent against state repression."

He elaborates how frequent FIRs and arrests wrongly accusing PTI activists of violence and vandalism during protests aim to deter support by criminalising dissent. "Whether demonstrating recently against blasphemous desecration of the Quran or the earlier Azadi March, police nominated myself and fellow workers in fabricated cases. But such terror tactics only strengthen our resolve. Non-violent civil disobedience remains the most potent weapon against tyranny."

Niaz avows determination to continue Khan's mission peacefully no matter the personal risks imposed by what he considers a rogue regime. "The imported government's panic is apparent -they indefinitely incarcerate our leader on concocted charges while attacking his character. But none of this can shake our conviction in his vision for real freedom and justice. Our families, now equally outraged at the trampling of rights, stand shoulder to shoulder in this decisive fight. Unity and courage is our strength no matter the oppression."

The passionate vows of youths like Niaz willing to sacrifice bright futures signal no hollow boast but a solemn oath shared by PTI cadres nationwide. With state excesses against Khan and his movement backfiring to swell resistance ranks, the illegitimate government's tenuous grip over judiciary, media and public opinion continues slipping. "Our leader's exemplary bravery and refusal to compromise has awakened the entire nation. Now the end is inevitable -we shall have our rights and freedoms restored under true democracy even if they imprison millions!"

Shab Niaz Khan further criticises Pakistan's entrenched two-party dynastic rule rotating power between Bhutto and Sharif families for decades, where both took turns plundering national wealth and blamed opponents once respective tenures ended through interventions.

He explains: "Since childhood, we only witnessed either Zardari mafia or Sharif brethren governing through kleptocracy and patronage, subverting state institutions for personal aggrandisement.

"Their conduct signalled Pakistan existed solely to enrich their offshore accounts and business empires. Selected leaders allowed free hand so long as they safeguarded military privileges and foreign policy dictates while keeping masses distracted through polarisation."

Further, Niaz argues: "Khan's meteoric rise directly threatened this status quo. Where previous figureheads dutifully protected the establishment, he pushed audacious reforms towards genuine democratisation and accountability. His ouster exposed collusion between political chess pieces and invisible hands. But awakened citizens now grasp the regime change conspiracy and illegitimacy of current contemptuous rulers illegally installed through foreign interference."

Niaz defiantly asserts: "Pakistan doesn't belong to any family inheritance or army proxies. Through our blood, sweat and votes, we civilians remain sole proprietors. The fervour around Imran Khan stems from his bold vision for reclaiming unconditional sovereignty and economic justice premised on redistributive state policies. No other leader ever combined patriotic intentions with competence and integrity as effectively. Whatever happens, we shall ensure he completes the mission founding fathers envisioned but successors failed."

Shab Niaz Khan lists pivotal reforms during Imran Khan's government benefitting citizens irrespective of ethnicity, further cementing cross provincial loyalty. Significant initiatives improving accessibility to education and jobs based on merit rather than privilege or bribery gave youths from humbler backgrounds unprecedented opportunities for social mobility.

He explains: "Khan mandated a standardised national curriculum raising education standards uniformly while increasing higher enrollment through need-based scholarships. Simultaneously PTI provincial government pioneered merit-based recruitments in Khyber Pakhtunkhwa through NTS examinations overturning the entrenched culture of cronyism in the public sector.

"These developments profoundly impacted Pashtun youth.

Talented students from our villages and valleys now gained a viable shot at higher studies and formal economy. Unlike past regimes doling out patronage and appointments to cronies, education and employment pathways opened based on merit rather than purchasing power. Such transparency enabled bright youths climbing out of poverty."

He continues: "By walking the talk on equitable access to public resources, Khan endeared himself to dispossessed populations. His vision rising above ethnic interests favours individual capability and national integration."

Niaz reaffirms unwavering support, proclaiming: "What Bhutto and Sharifs promised for decades without delivering, Khan implemented in KP and Center in few years despite resistance from mafias. His transformative governance benefiting masses explains the organic nationwide following rallying for his restoration. Unequivocally we declare -Pakistan stands with Imran Khan!"

For youth who never knew opportunity free from entanglement of class privilege, the "Naya Pakistan" dream holds visceral appeal. While previous generations submitted to inequality and nepotism as fate, Khan overturns oppressive determinism by introducing choice and dignity. Such a glimpse of a possible reality bonds the marginalised in solidarity behind the one leader daring to take on deeply vested archaic interests still controlling all levels of power.

4

"TRUTH IS THE POWER THAT WILL RESOLVE OUR PROBLEMS"

SEEKING TRUTH AND JUSTICE

Truth and justice have been defining traits of history's greatest leaders -from Prophet Muhammad (SAWW) and other prophets, to iconic religious figures across faiths. Truthfulness is a fundamental virtue that can elevate humanity, prohibiting wrongdoing when universally upheld. Speaking truth and living authentically are the first steps toward creating a more just world. If people collectively found the courage to speak uncomfortable truths, we could drive progress on even the most complex issues. For example, acknowledging the realities of the Palestinian struggle for sovereignty and the Kashmiri people's right to self-determination could be game-changing. Though the path to resolution is long, even small steps born of truth can spur positive momentum.

Beyond addressing injustice, truth enables human connection and understanding. Truth humanises situations rather than allowing misunderstanding to divide us. It removes ego and forced narrative, opening space for people to align around shared values and common ground. Truth and justice may seem lofty virtues, but embedding them into our everyday lives and interactions is the only way to build a society centred on these principles.

As an optimist, I believe in our collective potential to shape a more just world if we elevate truth as a core value. Even in darkness, the light of truth remains constant; we need only to turn towards it. There is no time to waste in collectively pursuing truth and justice.

Socrates valued truth and justice above all else. As a philosopher in ancient Athens, he frequently debated fellow citizens in the public square, challenging conventional thinking and championing logic over commonly held beliefs. Socrates was committed to uncovering universal truths rather than accepting perceived wisdom at face value. His relentless questioning aimed to expose ignorance and uncover deeper meanings.

As Socrates said: "The unexamined life is not worth living." He emphasised tirelessly pursuing truth through critical analysis and rational discourse.

Socrates' principles led him to be put on trial for supposedly corrupting Athenian youth and disrespecting the gods. When given the chance to escape execution, Socrates refused, determined to abide by his own teachings to the end. Even in his final moments, he stayed true to his beliefs, calmly drinking poison hemlock and dying a martyr for truth and justice against state oppression.

Socrates' courageous adherence to his principles set a defining example of remaining committed to core virtues despite the consequences. His teachings had an immense influence on civilisation, forming the foundation of western philosophy. Socrates demonstrated the transformative power individuals can have by living and speaking truthfully. His lasting legacy is a testament to the impact of reason, ethics and integrity.

Though Socrates paid the ultimate price for his beliefs, he

inspired others to likewise pursue truth and justice through rational examination and moral self-scrutiny. His example resonates through the ages as a reminder of the duty individuals have to uphold virtue, no matter the personal cost.

When I reflect on Imran Khan's struggle for truth and justice in fighting corruption in Pakistan, it evokes the pain and sacrifice of Socrates. Like Socrates, who questioned norms in ancient Athens, Khan has disrupted Pakistan's political status quo by speaking out against establishment players. After Khan was ousted as prime minister in April 2022, he alleged a US-backed conspiracy was behind his removal. Many criticised and ridiculed this claim. However, the recent Intercept report of 9 August 2023 lent credence to Khan's assertions.

According to the leaked diplomatic cable published by the Intercept, US officials met with Pakistan's ambassador in March 2022 and encouraged removing Khan over his neutral stance on Russia's invasion of Ukraine. The cable reveals the carrots and sticks the US deployed to pressure Pakistan to align with the US position against Russia. One month after the meeting, Khan was removed through a parliamentary vote of no-confidence. The sequence of events gives weight to Khan's accusations of a regime change conspiracy led by external powers.

While the truth remains contested, the leaked cable suggests Khan was punished for resisting external political influence, much as Socrates was persecuted for questioning Athenian authority. By persisting despite critics, Khan displayed philosophical courage in upholding his independent principles. The verdict of history remains to be seen, but Khan's struggle parallels the eternal battle between truth-speakers and powerful establishments.

Once again, Imran Khan has been vindicated in his scepticism of Gen. Bajwa and the military establishment. Khan had long warned that Bajwa was deceiving the people of Pakistan and could not be trusted. These allegations were dismissed by many as baseless conspiracies. However, the recent revelations about Bajwa's family amassing billions of rupees in assets during his tenure lend credence to Khan's mistrust.

According to reports, Bajwa's relatives became billionaires over six years, with assets totaling Rs 12.7 billion. This exorbitant enrichment occurred while Bajwa held the highest position of power in the nation. Khan had rightly questioned how the military chief's family could reap such fortunes without misconduct. While the full facts remain uncertain, the reports suggest Bajwa betrayed his office and the Pakistani people.

Once again, Imran Khan displayed philosophical courage in speaking uncomfortable truths about the powerful military apparatus. And once again, time has proven his integrity. Khan's struggle against what he perceives as corruption and deception evokes Socrates' eternal battle for wisdom and virtue against tyranny and hypocrisy. Though Khan has paid a price for his bold stance, history may look kindly on his willingness to challenge establishment narratives with inconvenient truths.

Despite the best efforts of his opponents, Imran Khan has yet to be proven guilty of any substantive wrongdoing against Pakistan and its people. The military establishment and its civilian allies have brought countless cases against Khan, but none have resulted in a credible conviction that would diminish his status as an honest leader.

Most recently, Khan and his PTI deputy Shah Mahmood Qureshi pleaded not guilty to charges related to Khan waving an alleged confidential document during a rally after his ouster. Khan maintains this unverified "cipher" proves his removal was orchestrated by the military and foreign powers, a claim they deny.

Though Khan faces legal challenges, the former cricket star still enjoys immense popularity and public trust. Even after being briefly jailed on controversial graft charges, then rearrested in the "cipher" case, the majority of the public stands steadfastly behind Khan. They recognise that the cases against him lack legitimacy and are attempts to tarnish his reputation.

Khan cannot currently participate in upcoming elections unless his convictions are overturned and his innocence affirmed. This highlights the importance of impartial due process to upholding truth and democratic principles. The public's unwavering support amid Khan's trials parallels the admiration many held for Socrates as he defended truth boldly against persecution by flawed systems of power and control. History often vindicates those who speak truth to power, regardless of consequences.

Truth, when intertwined with courage and bravery, becomes a powerful force. In my understanding, speaking the truth requires immense courage, especially in a nation that has been colonised for an extended period. True freedom, the kind that allows us to soar rather than crawl, can only be achieved by individuals with strong character traits, chief among them being the unwavering commitment to truth and fearlessness.

One of the most renowned examples of bravery in the history of Islam is Hazrat Ali (RA). Known for his indomitable spirit and valour, Ali (RA) fearlessly defended Prophet Muhammad (SAWW) in all battles, carrying his message with unwavering conviction. Born in Mecca and married to the daughter of Prophet Muhammad (SAWW), Ali's (RA) legacy lives on through his powerful quotes and the immense respect he commands for his fearlessness and truthfulness.

We cannot discuss truthfulness without mentioning the exemplary character of Prophet Muhammad (SAWW) himself. He was known throughout the Arab world as Sadiq (the Truthful) and Ameen (the Trustworthy), testaments to his unwavering commitment to truth and honesty. His life serves as an inspiration for all, and his teachings continue to guide individuals on the path of righteousness and integrity.

These exemplary figures from Islamic history serve as guiding lights for common men and women to learn from. Their bravery and truthfulness remind us of the importance of these virtues in our own lives. However, it saddens me to admit that only a small fraction of us truly focus on these virtues and strive to incorporate them into our daily lives.

In a world that often values convenience over honesty and fear over courage, it is crucial for us to reflect on the significance of truth and fearlessness. Speaking the truth requires strength and conviction, as it may challenge the status quo and invite resistance from those who prefer ignorance or deceit. Yet, it is only through the pursuit of truth and the courage to speak it that we can break free from the chains that bind us and truly embrace freedom.

Embracing truth and fearlessness not only liberates our own souls but also has the power to inspire and uplift those around us. By embodying these virtues, we become beacons of light in a world that sometimes feels dark and disoriented. Our actions and words carry the potential to shape and transform society, creating a ripple effect that spreads far beyond our immediate circles.

My leader always strives to follow in the footsteps of Hazrat Ali (RA), Prophet Muhammad (SAWW), and countless other brave individuals who have left an indelible mark on history through their unwavering commitment to truth and fearlessness. He has the courage to seek and speak the truth, even in the face of adversity, and his actions serve as a powerful reminder that truth and fearlessness are not mere ideals but powerful tools that can shape a more just and compassionate world.

My father was blessed with the traits of truthfulness and courage. He never compromised on speaking the truth, regardless of who he was dealing with. His uncompromising stance made some uncomfortable, including his superiors at work and influential members of our community. However, this did not deter my father. His face would become flushed red when pressured to be less blunt, yet he stood firm in his conviction. He would remind us:-it is Allah alone who sustains us, so why fear anyone else?

Since childhood, I have witnessed my father speak truth to power and face the consequences with resilience. Though I still have room to grow, I am fortunate to have inherited some of his disposition. As I document in my book, upholding truth requires bravery, especially when it clashes with conventional wisdom or those in authority. My father exemplified this through his words and deeds. I aim to carry forward his legacy, even if it comes at a cost. After all, truth has value in itself, regardless of who takes offence. With Allah's grace, I hope to live by the principles of my late father and my great leader.

When a nation is colonised for an extended period, the impacts of colonisation seep deeply into the fabric of society, even after formal independence occurs. The institutions, mentalities, and power dynamics established under colonial rule often persist, though the coloniser is now gone. In many ways, the roots planted by colonialism continue spreading through our collective psyche long after the colonisers have left.

Slavery, even mental slavery, slowly kills one's spirit and sense of freedom. We see this reflected in the famous story of the falcon raised among chickens. Having lived its formative years confined to a coop, the falcon had forgotten its innate ability to soar majestically through the skies. All it knew was the fearful, limited existence of the chickens around it.

Decades after independence, the chains of colonisation still weigh heavy on previously colonised peoples. When conditioned for generations to think small, contain yourself, and obey the coloniser's rules, it becomes difficult for a society to unlearn these mentalities overnight and truly take flight as a free people. The assumptions, behaviours, and norms ingrained under colonial rule persist, like the lingering trauma of abuse. True decolonisation is an ongoing process of examining our institutions, narratives, and social conditioning to root out the thorns left by colonialism. As Frantz Fanon wrote: "Decolonization is always a violent phenomenon." It requires dismantling so much of what was imposed on our ancestors. The work continues, but so must the deep belief in our inherent worth and freedom.

Imran Khan has consistently emphasised the need for Pakistanis to believe in their own freedom and sovereignty during his speeches. He insists that Pakistan's institutions must also have conviction in themselves and prioritise the nation's autonomy. Through his powerful rhetoric, Khan has aimed to help both the people and the government of Pakistan to break free from a 'slave mentality' and stop behaving like beggars.

When former prime minister Shehbaz Sharif made the controversial statement "Beggars cannot be choosers," it provoked strong backlash from Imran Khan and the wider public. Many felt offended, perhaps because Khan had reignited their sense of self-respect and reawakened feelings of freedom from dependency. The push for sovereignty and dignity that Khan championed made the notion of Pakistan as a "beggar" nation unacceptable to most.

In this way, Khan's emphasis on believing in Pakistan's self-worth and right to autonomy has reshaped mindsets. The offence taken at Sharif's words underscores the impact Khan had in boosting national pride and rejecting narratives of dependency. His vocal advocacy for freedom from foreign influence has resonated with many Pakistanis.

The quote "Bravery is standing with the truth and right" from Imran Khan directly reflects the vision he embodies and

the life he leads. Khan commonly motivates the people of
Pakistan with the statement "Khof kay botay tor do" (which
translates as: "Break the idols of fear") and stand united for a
just cause. His powerful words echo the rhetoric of many
influential leaders worldwide who have called on their nations
to conquer fear and uphold truth.

Khan has made courage in the face of adversity a central
theme of his messages and politics. By equating bravery with
adherence to truth and justice, his statements resonate with
Pakistanis seeking sincerity and integrity in their governance.
Khan presents standing up to fear and falsehood as a patriotic
duty. His frequent invocation to "Break the idols of fear"
inspires the nation to come together for change and reform.

In this way, Imran Khan's use of rhetorically evocative
language, drawing on historic archetypes of courageous
leadership, has rallied the Pakistani people around his
transformative vision. His speeches emphasise the need for
both bravery and principle in developing national unity and
pride. Khan's own bravery in confronting political dynasties
and vested interests has set an example many Pakistanis aspire
to follow.

I believe the kind of bravery Imran Khan displays stems
from an unshakeable faith --faith in one's self, in a higher
power, and in one's purpose. For Khan, his boldness is rooted in
his devoted connection to Allah. When our conviction is that
strong, it grants us the courage to speak truth to power.

To reach the level of leadership Khan has achieved requires
understanding and believing fully in one's cause. If we wish to
aspire to inspire billions, developing an exemplary character of
integrity and truthfulness is essential. The ability to stay true to
one's principles and values in the face of opposition is what
builds bravery.

Khan's fearless confrontations with dynastic political
families and entrenched interests is possible because of the

strength of his beliefs. For those who hope to follow in his footsteps, the first step is nurturing an unbreakable spirit of honesty and courage within. It is planting one's feet firmly in faith and purpose. With that foundation, standing firmly for the truth becomes second nature rather than a struggle.

Imran Khan represents the pinnacle of outspoken bravery combined with faith and conviction. To emulate his example requires cultivating those qualities within and letting them guide one's actions. The rest flows naturally when arising from that firm grounding of belief.

My father embodied such powerful beliefs throughout his life, even in his final moments. I vividly remember his unwavering conviction from two decades ago, when he was critically injured and fighting for his life in the ICU. Despite pressure from his brothers, my father steadfastly refused to falsely implicate innocent people for the shooting and would only name his actual attacker. Even gravely wounded, with bullets in his chest and liver, my father stayed true to his principles.

In a remarkable testament to forgiveness, he recorded a statement absolving his shooter and instructing my brother to focus solely on his and his sisters' education, including my own. My father maintained truth and integrity even while clinging to life, which only raises his stature more. I have no doubt that if my father were alive today to witness Imran Khan's valiant struggle, he would stand bravely alongside Khan's other fearless supporters. I often dream of my late father asking me about Khan's mission, which affirms his care and concern for my leader, even from heaven.

The memories of my father's courageous dignity, while enduring immense pain, will never fade. He embodied the same tireless commitment to truth and justice as Imran Khan. I see my father's spirit living on through this cause he would surely have made his own. His unwavering example continues inspiring me to stay the course with honesty and rectitude, no matter the circumstance.

Those who dedicate their lives to the pursuit of truth and justice achieve a form of immortality. Their spirits live on eternally because of the invaluable legacy they leave behind. While their physical bodies may perish, their principles and unwavering commitment echo through generations. Leaders who have the courage to stand up for what is right, no matter the personal cost, become symbols of hope and inspiration for all those who follow. Their incorruptible character and sacrifices for a noble cause are remembered and celebrated long after they are gone. These exemplars become the stuff of legend -their lives and deeds take on mythic proportions as lessons for humanity. In this way, leaders like Imran Khan, who stubbornly uphold honesty and boldly confront injustice, ensure their eternal relevance. Their souls are kept alive in the hearts and minds of their people. Their steadfast devotion to ethics serves as a moral compass, guiding their nation's future trajectory. While such principled leaders may face obstacles and opposition in their day, history ultimately vindicates them.

Therefore, the flame of truth lighting their journey can never be extinguished. Their immortal legacy persists to kindle that same fire in others. Those who live for truth and justice never really die -their light continues illuminating the way forward for generations yet unborn. Their memory and teachings are an eternal gift we inherit.

Courage of conviction is often bred from childhood through strong parenting and moral upbringing. The story of Moses illustrates this well. Moses was raised in the palace of the Pharaoh, surrounded by the power and opulence of Egypt's tyrannical ruler. Yet despite being adopted into Pharaoh's household, Moses embodied truth and justice.

This reveals how strength of character cannot be suppressed, even by an environment of corruption. Like a lotus flower blooming in muddy waters, Moses' noble spirit prevailed. His moral compass stayed true, though he was reared in a culture of oppression.

Moses' story shows how speaking truth to power is innate to those born with an unflinching spirit. No amount of privilege or palace conditioning could shake his steadfast commitment to justice. He defiantly confronted the man who had raised him because he would not compromise his principles.

Just as Moses was born with an unbreakable soul meant to deliver people to freedom, throughout history we see examples of saintly souls emerging even from criminal backgrounds. Nature's justice produces balancing forces --so where there is extreme injustice, sincerity is birthed to restore balance and truth.

Therefore, while positive parenting and upbringing nurture integrity, ultimately it is a quality ingrained at the soul level. No amount of external pressure can corrupt those destined to exemplify virtues like Moses did. Such brave hearts arrive in this world already equipped to face power with truth.

Imran Khan has demonstrated an indomitable spirit in the face of adversity throughout his life. Once he sets his sights on an objective, he pursues it indefatigably no matter the obstacles placed in his path.

As a champion cricketer, philanthropist, and now opposition leader, Khan has never capitulated in the face of challenges. Despite underhanded persecution from nefarious rivals seeking to maintain their nepotistic power, Khan soldiers on intrepidly. Echoing the grit of a stalwart captain determined to lead his team to victory, Khan rouses the people declaring: "Your captain will fight till the last ball." He remains unbowed and unbent by even the most insidious efforts to coerce him into acquiescence.

The reprehensible intimidation tactics against his loved ones cannot compel Khan to abandon his quest for reform. He embraces tribulation as a chance to exhibit valour. Khan's animating convictions are the wellspring of his dauntless spirit.

By exhorting his fellow citizens to keep hope alive, Khan breathes courage into their hearts. He disregards concerns for his safety to safeguard the aspirations of his people. Khan's audacious example in the line of fire ignites that same intrepid essence in the public.

In this way, Imran Khan has proven his mettle as a leader of adamantine integrity and pluck. His track record evidences that no matter how turbulent the billows, he will stay the course. Khan will march indefatigably forward for the greater good until his final breath. No perils or privations can quash the spirit of this paragon.

The true measure of courage is often tested in the face of adversity. Recently, a historic moment unfolded in Pakistan, as the trial of an accused individual is being held in a jail instead of a court, marking the first of its kind in the country's history. The proceedings are taking place in a small room within the premises of Adiyala jail, where only a handful of people can fit. Although this jail trial is not authorised by law, it serves as a powerful reminder that even in the most challenging circumstances, justice must prevail. Despite facing baseless charges against him, the strength of the accused, Khan, has exposed the weaknesses in the legal system. This serves as a stark reminder that even during the most challenging times, one individual can ignite the spark of change and inspire others to do the same. The significance of this jail trial could well be a catalyst for a much-needed overhaul of the legal system in Pakistan, paving the way for a more just and equal society.

Because of Khan's fear, the military establishment or the government controls every aspect of Pakistani media, and even his name is prohibited from being used by anyone there. This is a testament to the valour of one courageous man who has defeated a whole corrupt system. These ridiculous rules have never seen to be put into effect anywhere in the world as a whole in the twenty-first century, when free expression is valued highly. Fear spreads from his name to the PTI flag, and history is documenting how the Pakistani establishment and puppet government are illegally kidnapping, intimidating, beating, and detaining everyone who carries a PTI flag or even launches balloons with the party's colours on them. While such occurrences will always remain in our memories, the oppressive actions taken by the enemies of my leader and our nation demonstrate how the strongest leader in Pakistani history was able to topple the entire system.

Imran Khan has shown unwavering resolution, boldly proclaiming that "Even if I am left alone, I will continue fighting for true freedom and sovereignty. No one should misunderstand—no amount of pressure will ever make me step back from this purpose." His steadfast commitment speaks to the very ethos of persisting for what is right, regardless of opposition.

And indeed, the former prime minister will not stand alone. Heroes like Jehanzeb Paracha epitomise the solidarity Imran enjoys across all levels of loyalists willing to endure much for the cause of justice and Haqiqi Azadi.

Moreover, this is not merely one man's battle. Overwhelming solidarity evidenced by polls and surveys indicates nearly 80 per cent of the Pakistani nation promises never to withdraw backing from Imran Khan. For he represents the collective aspirations of the common citizens yearning to wrest back control of their beloved country.

This fight goes beyond party lines. It touches the very soul of the nation and its destiny ahead. The people see their own plight and dreams reflected in Imran's stand. His resistance gives voice to millions disenfranchised but still daring to chart a self-determined course.

And that collective hope will not be extinguished. Leaders like Imran Khan face prison and persecution precisely because the status quo knows the idea of Naya Pakistan lives vigorously in citizens' hearts, constantly threatening to turn ideals into reality. Intimidation aims to demoralise. But for every Jehenzeb punished for his bold stance on social media, a thousand more rally behind Imran, sending a clear message—we shall all soldier on together come what may!

The path ahead promises much suffering. But the people believe that this shared stand today will bear the fruit of Haqiqi Azadi tomorrow. That singular hope makes all tribulations worth enduring.

Jehanzeb Paracha's selfless commitment to advocating for true democracy in Pakistan through PTI began years before today's turmoil. He has actively volunteered with PTI UK's social media team since early 2018, contributing in a personal capacity initially.

But since April 2022, Paracha has significantly intensified his activism, spending substantial personal time and resources managing advocacy campaigns, amplifying voices of protest, and busting misinformation, all fuelled solely by an abiding love for Pakistan.

And Paracha is hardly alone. For every volunteer like him, there are thousands willing to sacrifice comforts because Khan's vision of independence, justice and empowerment resonates deeply with their hopes for Pakistan's future. These tireless activists power grassroots movements that mafia-like opposition groups fail to fathom. Unlike mercenaries fighting for short-term entitlements devoid of moral purpose, PTI supporters coalesce organically around shared convictions and emotional investments in reviving true democracy. For them, the cause transcends any single person; it is about reclaiming Pakistan's soul.

Still, standing up to entrenched authoritarian interests

comes fraught with risks, as the harrowing harassment of Paracha's own family demonstrates. But for volunteers irrevocably committed to principles now synonymous with Imran Khan's movement, neither intimidation nor slander can outweigh their stake in Pakistan's destiny. And side-by-side, they continue persisting despite profound personal costs, emboldened by hopes of victory heralding freedom's dawn.

We have seen supporters travelling across borders to physically back Khan, facing shelling and arrest risks outside his home. When asked what could warrant such self-endangerment, Paracha asserts: "The prize of a liberated homeland itself (is) enough incentive." After all: "Courage demands risks proportionate to the cause." And what "higher cause" exists than seeing one's motherland finally seize her destiny?

If the ideals of justice and democracy now wear the face of Imran Khan, so be it. For here stands the lone man still embodying the incorruptible spirit most felt lost. Every lathi blow, every jail door clanging, are 'small prices' to pay so their children inherit the Pakistan Jinnah envisioned: "unfettered by dynasts, unbroken in dignity".

Paracha understands: "Liberation tastes sweetest when earned, not granted." Unless masses reclaim rights surrendered, 1947's promise stays unfulfilled. If Khan alone keeps that promise alive, that proves enough. This dream has transcended personalities now. It marches, sits, bleeds, but still rises again. Always for Pakistan.

Some may condemn what they see as 'extreme' passions, cresting 'fearlessly against the citadels of oppression'. Paracha calls it duty. The greatest "jihad" lies in knowing what's truly worth "fighting for". What is "honour in inaction" while the homeland cries for "heroes to battle dark forces long ruling with impunity?" As he states: "Better to have stood and fallen than never stood at all when conscience commanded." By his creed, no cost outweighs: "The currency of clear conscience".

So critics can keep their hoarded comforts, paying lip service while acquiescing with kleptocrats. Let them mock as "dangerous" the ideals now animating resistance. The faithful have grafted Imran Khan's vision into their veins, pulses aligned to the heartbeat called Hope he resurrected. Their interlocked arms shield that heart's every beat. Together, they will breathe free in this Land of the Pure. Or not at all.

5

"WHAT I PERCEIVE IS ABOVE ALL JUSTICE, WHERE EVERYONE HAS THE SAME LAW"

IMPORTANCE OF MERIT AND RULE OF LAW

Imran Khan has often emphasised that removing consequences for merit and misconduct unravels social cohesion. He argues that properly rewarding good behaviour and punishing wrongdoing is essential for a healthy society. Khan's focus on accountability through rule of law is likely one reason he now faces legal prosecution and detention. But what exactly constitutes rule of law?

Rule of law means that government authority is exercised legitimately in accordance with written, publicly disclosed laws adopted through an open political process and enforced evenly through an accessible legal system. No one, including government officials, is above the law.

Laws should be clear, consistent, stable, applied evenly, and subject to public debate and scrutiny. They should protect basic human rights including liberty, due process, property rights, free speech and religion, equal treatment for all people, and access to justice. An independent judiciary is crucial to uphold the rule of law. Judges should be competent, ethical, and insulated from political or financial incentives. The courts enforce laws and check abuses of government power.

Equality before the law is an essential principle. Legal rights and protections must apply equally to all people regardless of status or connections. There should be no discrimination or preferential treatment under the law. Law enforcement agencies must also abide by the law, with institutional checks against illegal searches, detentions, excessive force, and other abuses of power.

The legal system should be accessible and affordable to all people. Barriers such as prohibitively high costs, delays, complex procedures, language hurdles, and distance from courts should be minimised. Alternative dispute resolution can provide efficient remedies but requires judicial oversight to protect rights. Corruption undermines the rule of law, so transparency, ethical oversight, and public participation help reduce undue influence.

Ongoing legal reforms may be needed to fully realise rule of law ideals in practice, through a legitimate democratic process. The core standard remains accountable to government under laws that are just, equally enforced, protective of human rights, and subject to independent judicial review. This upholds equality, fairness, and liberty for all people.

My leader says: "When you remove the concept of reward and punishment on merit, the result is the utter destruction of social fabric."

The essence of Khan's quote is that societies depend on systems of accountability that link rewards to merit and achievement, while also punishing poor conduct, rule-breaking and underperformance. He argues that removing consequences for good or bad actions erodes social cohesion and values.

In the quote, Khan suggests that having proper incentives and disincentives in place based on merit and adherence to rules is crucial for maintaining a strong, ethical society. Without tying rewards to hard work and talent, and penalties to laziness and misconduct, a society's sense of fairness and justice deteriorates. Individuals lose motivation to excel if achievement goes unrewarded. Wrongdoings multiply if left unpunished.

By invoking the "destruction of social fabric," Khan implies that dissolving connections between merit, ethics and consequences unravels the very bonds holding civilisation together. Right and wrong cease to matter in a world where neither is rewarded or penalised accordingly. His quote highlights the importance of accountability in human affairs and its foundational role in any well-functioning and just society.

The concept of divine reward and retribution is central to many faith traditions. In Christianity, Islam, Judaism and other religions, doctrines of heaven and hell promise eternal reward or punishment based on earthly conduct. The Bible and the Quran depict God rewarding virtue and punishing wickedness through these afterlives. Some interpret natural disasters and suffering as expressions of divine punishment.

At the same time, holy texts emphasise God's mercy, forgiveness, and opportunities for redemption. In Christianity, salvation through faith in Jesus is seen as overcoming the otherwise deserved punishment for sin. In Buddhism, poor karma accrued from wrongdoing leads to suffering, while good karma from virtue leads to rebirth in higher realms.

Beyond the afterlife, adherents believe God also rewards and punishes people in this lifetime. The Book of Proverbs in the Bible says that diligence and righteousness will be rewarded with prosperity, while misdeeds bring misery and misfortune. However, the innocent often appear to suffer while the wicked prosper, grappling faith in divine justice.

Nature itself can be seen as manifesting systems of reward and punishment. When ecosystems are cared for, they provide life-sustaining resources and beauty. When they are depleted and polluted, environmental degradation harms human health and quality of life. Some see this as the natural world rewarding good stewardship or punishing harmful actions.

In all, concepts of divine recompense and natural consequences underlie many faith traditions and perspectives. But how literally and fatalistically these are interpreted varies widely. Most theologies call for: responding to suffering with compassion, care for the vulnerable, and efforts to alleviate injustice --reflecting a balance of justice and mercy.

Parents commonly use rewards and consequences to reinforce positive behaviours in children while discouraging unwanted actions. Rewards like dessert, toys, screen time, or praise motivate children to complete chores, be kind to siblings, or achieve goals like potty-training. Mild punishments like time-outs or temporarily losing privileges teach accountability for tantrums, breaking rules, or hurting others. Finding the right balance teaches self-discipline.

Schools also implement reward systems to motivate student progress. High test scores or grades may bring praise from teachers, scholarships, enrollment in advanced classes, or privileges like free time. Punishments like detention, suspension or fines aim to curb plagiarism, truancy, bullying and other problematic behaviours. Clear conduct codes and fair procedures aim to maintain order.

Developmental psychology supports using a balance of rewards and consequences in child-rearing and education. Children's moral reasoning skills are shaped by experiencing results of right and wrong actions. And their brains are wired to prioritise behaviours that bring pleasure over pain. So linking desired actions to rewards, and undesired actions to proportional penalties, leverages basic human motivational drives.

However, experts caution against rewards and punishments becoming the sole motivators. Internal virtues like integrity, empathy and righteousness should also be instilled. And punishments should avoid being overly harsh or stifling self-direction. But overall, properly calibrated rewards and consequences teach accountability, ethics, and responsible decision-making -helping children become productive members of society. So in moderation and with wisdom, they remain effective parenting and educational tools.

Imran Khan often grounds his positions in philosophical principles and historical examples. His advocacy for rule of law stems from deeply-held beliefs about social justice. Khan attempted to demonstrate accountability himself by voluntarily submitting to legal proceedings. Nonetheless, his critics contend Khan struggled to consistently implement rule of law within his own party. There were allegations of corruption against some PTI party members that went unaddressed. This apparent selective accountability fuelled accusations of hypocrisy and double standards.

While Khan enacted some reforms, the lack of action against alleged misconduct in his own ranks cost him credibility and public trust. Failures to censure party officials for alleged corruption contradicted Khan's vocal stances against graft. This lost him some supporters who had grown disillusioned.

In principle, Khan expressed beliefs in transparency, ethics in government, and across-the-board accountability. But putting these into practice proved challenging. The perceived failure to clean up corruption within his own party violated the very ideals Khan championed. This remains a criticism of his term as prime minister.

Yet, governing is often more complex than philosophical principles. No leader achieves perfect alignment between ideals and implementation. Khan faced opposition and competing priorities that muddied plans for reform. But the goal of impartial rule of law remains vitally important for

Pakistani democracy. With effort and wisdom, greater progress can perhaps be made.

As earlier stated, even great leaders are human and inevitably make mistakes at times. A hallmark of wise leadership is acknowledging and learning from errors in judgement.

Since his ouster in the regime change, Imran Khan has demonstrated such reflective leadership. He has openly admitted misplacing his trust in certain party members who later betrayed him. Rather than denying or downplaying these errors, Khan has taken accountability for misjudgements in placing confidence in individuals who proved unworthy. While no leader can perfectly assess loyalty or character, owning up to putting faith in the wrong people reveals maturity and integrity. By publicly accepting this mistake, Khan aims to grow as a leader and prevent repeat errors in assessing who to trust in the future.

None of this excuses the opportunism of those who betrayed Khan for selfish aims after receiving his patronage. The blame for disloyalty rests fully on them. But Khan's frank admission of his own mistake shows laudable humility and transparency.

His reflection also reinforces that even skilful leaders can sometimes rely on those who lack principles. Admitting this helps Khan recommit to surrounding himself with figures of wisdom, ethics, and dedication to Pakistani democracy. Overall, acknowledging even painful errors demonstrates Khan's resolve to learn and improve -qualities that differentiate great leaders.

In countries like Pakistan, the powerful elite are seldom held accountable to the law. So Imran Khan's conviction over the Toshakhana case, despite flaws in the trial, demonstrates the uphill struggle to implement rule of law.

Khan was jailed by Judge Dilawar in a rushed verdict later

deemed improper by the Islamabad High Court itself. The unjust haste and disproportionate sentence furthered perceptions of a politicised prosecution targeting Khan. This exemplifies the dual justice system in Pakistan --one for the influential and connected, and one for those who confront the status quo. The flawed trial process and conviction on exaggerated charges underscores Khan's challenge in advocating rule of law over elite privilege.

However, the fact that an appellate court intervened to suspend the suspect's sentence shows that progress is possible. With sustained reform and integrity within the judiciary, the justice system can move towards equitability. But Khan's ordeal reveals just how entrenched opposition to accountability remains among vested interests. Despite setbacks, Khan deserves credit for spearheading this fight. His courage sets an example of speaking truth to power. Delivering fair and transparent rule of law for all in Pakistan will be an ongoing struggle. But Khan has shaken the discourse towards greater consciousness of this democratic necessity.

Imran Khan has been selectively targeted for prosecution over the Toshakhana gifts while others escape accountability for similar practices. However, in igniting this debate, Khan has provoked broader demands for transparency and rule of law across Pakistani institutions.

Khan's conviction over Toshakhana gifts appears disproportionate when military leaders and politicians across parties enjoy untold wealth without scrutiny. The questionable trial exposes bias in a system that punishes Khan while shielding more powerful figures.

However, Khan's bold stand has sparked national outrage at this double standard. His willingness to face injustice has awoken Pakistani citizens to demand wholesale accountability. Growing calls for transparency from all sectors, including the military, reflect this influence. Recent questioning of COAS

Bajwa's finances suggests the populist pressure Khan's struggle catalysed. Though Khan personally suffers, his sacrifice has pulled the mask off untouchable elites. This national awakening to corruption may prove Khan's enduring legacy, even if flawed prosecutions seek to tarnish his image.

Of course, those with vested interests attempt to silence dissent and cling to privilege. But Khan has primed the public to scrutinise the powerful like never before. The genie of transparency cannot easily return to the bottle. Thus, despite an unfair predicament, Khan's trial has, ironically, advanced his democratic reform agenda. The road ahead remains long, but his resilience against injustice has inspired a movement. Khan's willingness to weather the fire of retaliation has ignited a national reawakening --one that now holds all leaders to account.

Imran Khan not only charged into the proverbial lion's den by targeting elite privilege,-but he also flung open the doors to allow public scrutiny of long-hidden corruption. For this, he faces consequences that the powerful find unbearable.

Khan did not stand alone, but alongside daring journalists willing to expose hard truths and hold the untouchable accountable. Chief among them was Arshad Sharif, shot dead in Kenya after being forced into exile for his uncompromising integrity. His blood stains those who silenced the truth he exposed.

Others, like Imran Riaz Khan, also sacrificed liberty and livelihood to endorse facts over propaganda. The abduction and detention of these critical voices aims to intimidate, but echoes of suppressed narratives persist. Such repression reveals precisely why the privileged fear Khan and his crusade for transparency. But his struggle marches forward. With perseverance and solidarity, the light of justice dims even the most deep-rooted darkness. It is a steep climb, but Khan has set the wheels of accountability in motion. His courage inspires citizens to believe they, too, can redeem democracy. And he stands on the shoulders of journalistic giants, whose sacrifices paved the path for Pakistan's advancement. The nation owes heroes like Arshad Sharif eternal gratitude for shining light on corruption -their torch now carried forth by Khan. The struggle endures for courageous voices like Moeed Pirzada, Sabir Shakir, Wajahat Saeed Khan and others now reporting from abroad. Forced to flee for their safety, they nonetheless persist in providing facts that combat false narratives. Their work upholds a proud legacy of Pakistani journalists who place truth above self-interest. The nation eagerly awaits the full recovery of Imran Riaz Khan, abducted for daring to challenge the untouchable. His absence leaves an immense void. May he regain his health and platform soon. These journalists make monumental sacrifices, but their steadfast commitment to transparency in dark times kindles hope. Their fierce integrity inspires citizens to stay the course alongside leaders like Imran Khan.

Despite immense pressure, a diverse coalition of supporters persists in advancing Imran Khan's vision of rule of law and accountability. Even with the powerful elite attempting to crush dissent, countless patriotic Pakistanis remain united behind Khan's democratic struggle. Prominent PTI supporters like Sanam Javed, Tayyaba Raja, Aliya Hamza alongside other female prisoners, inspire women to take a stand. Dedicated journalists combat falsehoods despite great personal risk. Grassroots activists and PTI's social media army work tirelessly to organise and inform.

Among the victims of state oppression in Pakistan are courageous female supporters of Imran Khan's PTI party. Many were subjected to unjust imprisonment over flimsy charges related to peaceful protests. Even more disturbing are reports of security personnel brutally manhandling female protesters - dragging them by their hair and clothes during PTI rallies, leaving many traumatised. Such heavy-handed measures against women for simply exercising their democratic rights violates human dignity. It has drawn global condemnation but has not deterred these brave females from continuing their struggle. Their resilience against intimidation tactics reveals the bankrupt morality of those who sanction violence against peaceful citizens. Even if the sky falls, their commitment remains unshaken.

This diverse populist movement, armed only with truth, has withstood arrests, threats and violence. Their nonviolent resistance exposes the fascism of opaque figures who flout the law to preserve privilege. Together with Khan, this awakened citizenry chips away at secrecy and corruption.

No doubt, the road ahead remains arduous. But this coalition, reflecting all sections of society, has shattered the aura of invincibility around embedded elites. Their bravery rekindles hopes for a truly democratic Pakistan, governed by rule of law. Come what may, this united front will soldier on until transparency and accountability become reality. Their willpower carries forward the vision Khan boldly champions from behind bars.

The drama on 9 May surrounding Imran Khan's court hearing was a disgraceful episode. PTI workers peacefully protesting were brutally attacked by unknown assailants, leaving many injured. Meanwhile, inside the courtroom, Khan himself was subjected to unacceptable mistreatment, being dragged and shoved by security forces. His legal team was obstructed from their lawful duties. The entire debacle resembled a scene from a dictatorship, not a democracy. It was likely a deliberate attempt to provoke tensions and project Khan's supporters as violent. This false narrative only amplifies calls for transparent rule of law. The heavy-handedness shows the insecurity of elites fearful of Khan's principled leadership.

But such thuggery will neither deter peaceful protest nor derail demands for democratisation. The truth cannot be suppressed.

As Imran Khan says, true freedom entails struggle and sacrifice. In the two years since his ouster, patriotic Pakistanis have embodied this truth by giving their all for rule of law and sovereignty. Their courage awakens the nation's conscience.

Chief among the victims of state oppression was Ali Bilal, affectionately known as Zill-e-Shah. Zill-e-Shah was a spirited man who faced mental health challenges. However, he found joyful purpose supporting PTI rallies. Though the political intricacies exceeded his comprehension, Zill-e-Shah cherished the welcoming atmosphere at PTI gatherings. He developed a childlike adoration for Imran Khan. Tragically, Zill-e-Shah was arrested and tortured to death in custody simply for his innocent PTI affiliation. The sheer brutality against this gentle soul exposes the monstrous cruelty of the forces working to silence PTI. But it has only strengthened the resolve of millions of Pakistanis. Zill-e-Shah's memory now symbolises the human cost of tyranny, fuelling the struggle for freedom and justice he loved.

Other party workers also attained martyrdom while voicing dissent. Their blood irrevocably stains those who sanctioned such brutality just to silence demands for transparent democracy. But these sacrifices will not be forgotten, nor their mission abandoned.

The entire nation owes profound gratitude to these souls lost in defiance of tyranny. Their light guides Pakistan towards the vision of justice, accountability, and freedom, embodied by leaders like Imran Khan. Achieving this ideal remains difficult, but not impossible, with such inspirational examples of selfless courage.

No doubt my father, if alive, would've happily sacrificed his life on Khan's mission. Countless patriotic Pakistanis today see

Khan as the singular leader committed to saving Pakistan through transparent democracy and rule of law.

Other political figures treat governance as a revolving door for personal enrichment, fleeing abroad when power slips away. Their self-interest contradicts Khan's sincere attachment to Pakistan as his home to live and die for. The public recognises that while Khan may not be perfect, his fierce devotion to reforming the corrupt system comes from an authentic place of patriotism. He prioritises national interest over personal gain.

This contrast explains the groundswell of popular support for Khan, despite the state's repression. The public sees him as their only anchor of hope against the ruling elites bleeding Pakistan dry. The establishment fails to grasp this source of Khan's appeal. While they may temporally overpower him, they cannot extinguish the aspirations of millions of citizens now awoken to their democratic rights and agency. Rain or shine, Khan has already permanently transformed the nation's political consciousness. This movement he sparked for genuine democracy, justice, and sovereignty will only grow. Its torch shall be carried forward by devoted patriots like my leader until fulfilled.

Gul Zafar Khan, hailing from the merged Bajaur district, recounts the blood-curdling night when forces barged into his home, ransacking everything in sight. "But it was seeing my nine-year-old special needs son dragged away screaming that shattered my soul," shares former PTI MNA (Member of National Assembly), eyes moistening. This brazen kidnapping of an innocent speech-impaired child gained immense media attention as Khan desperately sought his safe return.

The cold indifference from the police station just 100 metres away felt equally gutting afterward. Despite the case making headlines across Pakistan after frantic social media outreach, not one officer even feigned a cursory probe or investigation into the abandoned child's recovery.

Horrifyingly, such incidents have become almost commonplace under the current regime. Khan laments how, over the last 20 months since Imran Khan's ousting, countless children have been detained as leverage to pressure parents supporting PTI. Even disabled people aren't spared, like Zille Shah, a mentally-challenged man arrested without charge. His mutilated corpse later surfaced with signs of unspeakable torture. "What threat can a helpless man like that pose to the state's might?" asks Khan bitterly.

And yet, giving up is no option when the nation's future hangs in the balance. Khan asserts matter-of-factly: "I am Pakhtun. Independence and self-respect breathe life into our lungs." His ancestors resisted British imperialists; facing current tyrants trying to crush dissent seems less frightful in that context. Still, his wife, and other women in his family now rarely step outdoors unattended, their very sense of security shattered. Fists clenched, Khan repeats that the regime has sunk lower than the enemy sparing women and children in war.

Recalling the harrowing raid, his tone toughens, recounting how forces barged in like thieves, ransacking his home with guns blazing. "After me? Fine. But what threat poses a speech-impaired nine-year old?" Fury rising, Khan describes the ruthless snatching of his special-needs son -a helpless child too disabled to even comprehend the violence unleashed.

"As any father would, I love my son deeply --especially one with such innocence and dependency. So they targeted my heart, plain and simple." The cold indifference afterward, he remarks, felt equally gutting, as not one officer even feigned a cursory investigation despite appeals to recover the terrified kid abandoned roadside.

When asked whether this flagrant intimidation weakens his

resolve, Khan scoffs as though the question itself is absurd. "I'm Pakhtun --independence and self-respect breathe life into our lungs. My forefathers battled British imperialists once; facing petty tyrants hardly compares. Who threatens women and children other than cowards defeated and desperate?" sighs Khan, wearily.

Yet quitting PTI never even crosses his mind. If anything, outrage against such bullying only fans the popularity of Khan's campaign, which promises to restore sanity. "Countless workers already sacrificed life and liberty for Naya Pakistan's dream --compared to their trials, I've given nothing." No matter how many heads get cracked, he asserts PTI loyalists will keep flooding the streets, their leader's iron will infused in their veins.

"I think Imran Khan's biggest weakness was his blind faith in the country's constitution. He made every political move believing the judiciary would support it since none of his decisions were unconstitutional --whether dissolving assemblies or demanding immediate elections. But the powerful elite clearly consider the constitution as nothing more than a piece of paper while the judiciary stands unable to implement any decision," asserts Khan, frustratedly.

No matter, he maintains the PTI fight goes on. His message to party workers and supporters is clear: "Nothing lasts forever, there will be a full stop to this barbarism one day, God willing. Keep yourself ready for elections and we shall answer these brutal tactics at the ballot box!"

Because they understand what the detractors don't --that rare, selfless visionaries battling entrenched mafias come but once in generations. So no matter the personal costs, backing Imran Khan stands as a greater duty towards the future. Certainty of triumph or failure matters less than having stood up today for Pakistan's soul when conscience commanded it.

Most PTI leaders and supporters remain peaceful and are

seeking change through constitutional means, despite provocation. Brutal police crackdowns, arrests of members, and even the alleged abduction of an ex-MNA's disabled child fail to break the party's non-violent stance. Across prisons crammed with workers, and leaders defiantly raising slogans for Haqeeqi Azadi, a singular message emerges from PTI's ranks: revenge awaits; not through might, but the ballot alone. This commitment to achieving change through elections above all demonstrates Imran Khan's transformative impact on Pakistan's political landscape. Under traditional feudal parties, outrage over similar state excesses would have ignited calls for violent retaliation and exploited public fury. Yet PTI disciplines even grief into a collective determination to triumph at the polls, no matter what injustices get inflicted along the way by panicked opponents.

Acknowledging the provocations mounting daily, Khan insists on compassing response to only legal and democratic options. The refusal to be goaded into extra-constitutional actions itself signifies PTI's readiness to assume power. This sharp contrast against violent opposition tactics highlights the progressive vision which has captured the imagination of millions dreaming of a prosperous, liberated Pakistan.

Indeed, the defiant non-violence stems from a moral authority signalling the dawn of a new Pakistan. Past rulers traditionally cultivated patronage through brute force, but PTI stakes political capital by absorbing blows without retaliation. This signals clearly to allies and adversaries alike that the PTI reign shall ring in where no citizen need fear unjust persecution by the state.

The commitment to seek justice for victims, like the disabled child cruelly ripped from his home, tells all aggrieved groups that their trauma will be acknowledged and addressed under PTI. That no manner of cruelty against party members can dilute its pledge to provide insaaf once elected, reinforces its appeal across marginalised segments as Pakistan's only leading national party bridging ethnic and religious divides.

By enduring the vicious backlash against his vision stoically, Khan has nurtured a movement which responds to grave rights violations through the robust democratic process instead of counter-productive violence. Pakistan's alienated youth, often vilified as rage-filled mobs, now better channel their frustrations productively, due to PTI's organised platforms.

The refusal to abandon constitutional methods despite rampant abuse of authority illustrates a central pillar for Naya Pakistan --establishing rule of law, applied evenly. Abnormalities represent rejection of circumstantial exceptions to upholding justice. PTI's historic rise proved institutions alone cannot squash people-led movements anchored in strong moral conviction. Whether or not stolen elections get restored, history has already recorded this society's peaceful defiance, sparked by one leader's unbending stand of Haq against Baatil.

6

"NEVER GIVE UP, NO MATTER HOW HARD LIFE GETS, NO MATTER HOW MUCH PAIN YOU FEEL"

CULTIVATING PERSISTENCE AND RESILIENCE

R esilience and persistence are indispensable traits for effective political leadership. In the chaotic realm of politics, leaders face a ceaseless barrage of problems, attacks, and crises that would overwhelm many. Political leaders must demonstrate extraordinary resilience --the ability to recover from setbacks and press forward. They need tremendous persistence to keep working toward their vision despite constant obstacles. Politicians lacking resilience are in danger of being broken by the immense pressures inherent to governance. Criticism and resistance are unavoidable in the political arena. Resilient leaders let such hardships roll off their backs. They do not take negativity personally or let it fracture their confidence. Instead, they maintain optimism and focus on solutions. Voters trust resilient leaders to remain steady during turmoil.

Persistence allows political leaders to stay the course, pursuing their long-term policy goals. They cannot accomplish systemic change quickly, or without opposition. Persistent leaders are willing to incrementally chip away at intractable problems. They work tirelessly to build coalitions, revising strategies but never giving up on their core aims. Voters know persistent leaders will fight for their interests year after year.

Both resilience and persistence stem from a leader's sense of purpose and principles. Values-driven leaders can endure almost any criticism and obstacle because they act with conviction. Their resilience and persistence signal authenticity, and integrity to constituents. This builds loyal grassroots support that sustains political leaders through the inevitable ups and downs of their careers.

In these hyperpartisan times, resilience and persistence enable political leaders to withstand poisonous divisiveness. Resilient leaders do not escalate conflict. Their persistence focuses on common ground, not partisan rancour. Voters long for public servants who can restore civility and make government functional again.

The challenges facing our nation demand political leaders with unusual resilience and persistence. Problems like economic inequality, climate change, and injustice can seem intractable. To spearhead lasting solutions, leaders must have the emotional fortitude to recover from defeats, and the determination to keep driving toward progress. Voters will empower leaders with the resilience and persistence to deliver meaningful change.

Throughout history, great leaders have demonstrated remarkable resilience and persistence in the face of adversity. Their ability to recover from setbacks and keep pursuing their goals enabled them to achieve profound, positive change.

In the Christian faith, Pope John Paul II epitomized resilience and persistence. Born in 1920s Poland under oppression, he endured Nazi occupation, lost his family by age 20, and lived under Soviet communist rule. Despite such hardship, he clung to his Catholic beliefs and became an influential bishop. As Pope during the 1980s, he persisted in the face of opposition from communism. His resilience and dedication helped inspire the Polish people's Solidary movement, contributing to the eventual fall of the Soviet Union.

Civil rights icon Martin Luther King Jr. showed astonishing resilience as he repeatedly faced violence, bomb threats, unjust jailing, and public criticism. Police assaulted him many times during protests, yet he refused to respond to hatred with violence. His persistence through setbacks was key to major milestones like the Montgomery bus boycott and the March on Washington. Both his resilience and faith-driven persistence energised the broader freedom movement.

Turning to the political realm, Abraham Lincoln lost eight elections before becoming president of the fracturing United States. Despite repeated defeats, he never gave up on his vision for America. His resilience buoyed him through deep personal losses and the overwhelming trials of the Civil War. Lincoln's persistence paid off when he achieved emancipation and began reunifying the nation.

Former South African president, Nelson Mandela, demonstrated almost inhuman resilience during 27 years imprisoned for his anti-apartheid activism. He channelled the rigors into an opportunity for growth, strengthening his commitment to equality. As the country's first post-apartheid president, his astonishing persistence through decades of setbacks enabled him to unify both white and black South Africans.

Prominent British prime minister, Winston Churchill, was defined by his gritty resilience during the second world war. Despite a string of early military defeats, Churchill refused to surrender. His memorable speeches fortified British resilience throughout the London Blitz bombings. Churchill's persistence led Great Britain through its darkest hour into eventual victory.

Turning to eastern faiths, the Dalai Lama has lived in exile for over 60 years after China seized Tibet. Despite being unable to return home, he continues travelling the world campaigning for Tibetan autonomy and teaching Buddhist values of compassion. His resilience stems from a deep spirituality while persistence in his political cause remains nonviolent.

Indian civil rights pioneer Mahatma Gandhi weathered many setbacks over decades before gaining independence from Britain. Jailed frequently for nonviolent protests, he would emerge more resilient each time. For over 50 years, he peacefully persisted in the liberation movement. Gandhi's resilience and persistence profoundly inspired India and many other post-colonial struggles.

Modern political resilience and persistence were on display during Democrat Nancy Pelosi's first term as the first-ever female speaker of the United States House of Representatives. She persisted through bitter partisan attacks and scepticism about her historic speakership. Pelosi demonstrated political resilience by regaining the speaker role a decade later. Her persistence on major reforms like the Affordable Care Act made an enduring impact.

Republican Senator John McCain's political resilience was shaped by years as a prisoner of war in Vietnam. In Congress he became known for persisting through bitter policy fights, despite criticism from his own party. McCain's willingness to work across party lines demonstrated essential resilience at a time of deepening partisan divides.

The world recently watched young climate activist Greta Thunberg persist in calling for climate action despite initial mockery and attacks. Her resilience and principled persistence sparked a global youth climate movement. She exemplifies how passionate persistence, backed by resilience, can catalyse social change.

Former New Zealand prime minister, Jacinda Ardern, has won international praise for her resilient, persistent leadership through these turbulent times. Her empathy and focus united

New Zealanders through the Christchurch mosque attacks and the global pandemic. Ardern's poise under pressure demonstrates that resilience and compassion can overcome even monumental challenges.

The diverse stories of these resilient, persistent leaders across eras and domains reveal some shared traits that enable one to thrive amid adversity: faith in their cause, moral conviction, emotional intelligence, and growth mindset. Their legacies lend hope that, with the right mindset and strength of spirit, the most persistent problems of our world can eventually be overcome.

My father exhibited remarkable resilience and persistence in empowering his daughters through education, despite facing criticism. He staunchly supported sending me and my sisters to school, unlike most families in our traditional community at the time. Facing pressure from relatives, he persisted in the belief that girls deserve the same opportunities as boys.

Showing equal resoluteness at home, my father taught me to ride a bicycle, and let me wear jeans and t-shirts as a child. This was unheard of for a girl in our highly patriarchal society in the 1980s. His resilience in the face of cultural norms gave me the confidence to push boundaries and be myself. While seen as defiant by some, my father remained focused on nurturing his daughters' potential. His resilience stemmed from moral conviction. He once told me: "Never let others dictate what you can or cannot do." That lesson instilled in me a spirit of persistence that has served me well in all endeavours.

I feel fortunate to have had a father who championed me. His resilience in upholding progressive values shaped me into an empowered woman. I aim to exhibit that same persistence in expanding opportunities for the next generation, much like my leader, Imran Khan. Through political resilience and unwavering persistence, Imran Khan has inspired millions of Pakistani youth to believe they can achieve great things. My father taught me resilience on a personal level, while Imran Khan embodies it on a national scale. I strive to mirror their tenacity in everything I do, empowering others while never giving up on my vision of a more just society. With role models like my father and Imran Khan, I am optimistic that progress will prevail through persistence.

Imran Khan's lifelong resilience and persistence have enabled him to achieve seemingly impossible goals against incredible odds. His journey from cricket champion to philanthropist, to prime minister of Pakistan, is a testament to the power of perseverance.

Imran Khan's determination and relentless work ethic fuelled his rapid rise in cricket from his early years. He first played for his school's cricket team as a pace bowler in 1962 at age nine, while attending Aitchison College in Lahore. His skills developed throughout the 1960s, representing various club and collegiate sides.

Khan made his Test cricket debut against England in 1971 at Edgbaston. In 1976, he returned to Pakistan and secured a permanent place on the national team. During the late 1970s, Khan was one of the pioneers of the reverse swing bowling technique. He also has the second-highest all-time batting average of 61.86 for a Test batsman playing at position 6 in the batting order.

Khan took over the captaincy of the Pakistan cricket team in 1982 till his retirement.

Between 1976-1978, a series of stress fractures threatened to end his meteoric career. Each time, doctors predicted he would never bowl again at an elite level. Demonstrating remarkable resilience, Imran courageously underwent rehabilitation and reinvented his bowling style, returning to play each time.

Imran's most brilliant achievement came in 1992, when he captained Pakistan to victory in the ICC Cricket World Cup at age 39, capping his illustrious 20-year career. Despite naysayers claiming he was past his prime, Imran marshalled his skills one final time to lift the trophy in Australia.

Retiring from cricket, Imran embarked on a philanthropic mission to establish a cancer hospital in Lahore, after his mother's death from the disease in 1985. Starting fundraising in 1991, Imran persisted for over two decades to turn his vision into reality. In 1994, he registered his charity as the Shaukat Khanum Memorial Trust, named after his mother. After immense struggle, the first specialised cancer hospital finally opened in 1994.

Shifting his persistence toward politics, Imran officially founded the PTI party in 1996 to fight corruption and cry for reform. For the next 15 years, he resiliently grew his grassroots movement while facing enormous resistance from Pakistan's political elite. His persistence finally achieved victory in 2018, when PTI won the national elections, leading to Imran being sworn in as prime minister in August 2018 at age 65.

Imran Khan's lifelong resilience and tireless persistence through oft-insurmountable odds make him a nationally revered figure in Pakistan across generations. He exemplifies that one person's self-belief and determination can defy expectations, overcome obstacles, and achieve the impossible.

Imran Khan has demonstrated unwavering resilience throughout his life, overcoming great obstacles to achieve remarkable feats. As the prime minister, he has faced unprecedented challenges, enduring relentless persecution from opposition forces. Despite these trials, Imran has remained steadfast and resolute in his determination to lead with integrity and honour.

Following his victory in the 2018 election, Imran Khan and his party, PTI, faced significant opposition from the political elite, who had long been in power in Pakistan. The PTI's rise to power was seen as a threat to the established order, and the old guard were quick to take action in order to undermine the fledgling government. This included a campaign of harassment, arrests, and torture, aimed at breaking the resolve of the PTI and its supporters. The situation was tense, and the future of the government was uncertain, as it struggled to maintain its grip on power amidst fierce resistance from the entrenched establishment.

In 2022, the opposition tried forcing Imran's loyal party members to defect against him. Though some acquiesced under extreme pressure, Imran stood resilient in denouncing these illegal and unethical tactics. The final straw was a failed assassination attempt in November 2022, while Imran was leading a rally. Though injured, Imran was defiant in resuming his march more galvanised than before. His enemies had failed to intimidate him into submission.

Through this turmoil, Khan has channelled his sportsman's stoicism, drawing resilience from his faith and principles. The political mafia underestimated his courage and conviction. Their persecution has only expanded Imran's support from ordinary citizens rallying around this rare leader who cannot be broken.

Now deposed unfairly, Imran persists undaunted in his struggle for justice and democratic rights, backed by throngs of passionate followers. His resilience in the face of political oppression is forcing a reckoning with the corrupt status quo. Imran emerges stronger from every challenge, proving his is a long game requiring perseverance. His unbroken spirit continues fuelling a movement demanding genuine change.

Imran Khan's lifelong resilience and fearless persistence is forcing Pakistan's entrenched political order to panic. Intimidation only spurs this singular leader toward purpose. Imran's indomitable grit is inspiration that with courage and perseverance, justice and progress can defeat even the greatest obstacles. While exuding remarkable resilience, Imran Khan has also shown his human side when supporters close to him are unjustly targeted.

In 2022, police forces ransacked Imran's home and harassed his wife, Bushra Bibi, with vindictive legal cases. In rare visible dismay, Imran denounced the violation of his family's basic rights.

Imran Khan's nemesis in Pakistan's establishment or Pakistan's government have pulled out all the stops trying to fracture his spirit. First deposed unfairly as prime minister, he was then hit with fabricated court cases to bar him from politics.

Despite being denied the right to defend himself in court, Imran remained steadfast, warning of a massive uprising if silenced. Undeterred, the politicised courts raced to convict Imran in an absurd cipher case; concocted, perhaps, by the military elite.

Sentenced without due process, Imran has been subjected to inhumane imprisonment. Confined alone in a tiny cell, he is deprived of proper sleep and exercise. In an insidious attempt to mentally torment him, his jailers have allegedly poured sweet liquid onto the floor to attract swarms of ants and other insects. Imran withstands these devious humiliations with quiet resilience. The petty cruelties inflicted on him only highlight the injustice and corruption plaguing the entire legal proceedings. Though his captors try to break him in both body and spirit, Imran remains unyielding in his dignity.

Yet relentless persecution has only expanded Imran's support. Record crowds gathered, demanding his freedom. In jail, Imran's dignity and resilience exposes the sham legal proceedings against him. No establishment intimidation can subdue his dream of justice.

Imran endures these unlawful hardships as a political prisoner, well aware of the cruel fate faced by so many innocents in Pakistan's corrupt justice system. His personal suffering only deepens his commitment to reform.

Far from breaking his spirit, Imran's unjust ordeal has awakened masses to the authenticity of his struggle. As with giants like Nelson Mandela, imprisonment has forged Imran Khan as an enduring symbol of resilience against tyranny. His oppressors have already lost.

Imran has also advocated tirelessly for female party members, jailed for months on fabricated charges. Though resilient in his own right, Imran's sense of justice compels him to fight for these wrongfully imprisoned women.

When loyal PTI organiser Zille Shah was murdered, Imran grieved this young activist silenced by violence. His empathy shows that behind his own stoicism, Imran deeply values supporters who have risked everything for his movement.

While attacks aim to fracture Imran's spirit, they reveal his care for the vulnerable. Imran insists his struggle is for Pakistan's future, not personal glory. His rare resilience stems from this higher purpose -to build a just society for the coming generations.

Imran persists undaunted by any personal cost. But he continues drawing resilience from the supporters who have placed their hopes in him. Their shared quest for reform strengthens his resolve that together, against all odds, a brighter dawn will come for Pakistan.

Syed Hamza Shah seemed destined for great success --the young, ambitious entrepreneur steadily built his start-up into a leading urban development firm in Pakistan's bustling capital, leveraging smooth charm and bold vision equally prized in boardrooms and political halls.

Yet today, Shah sits confined to the narrow defendant's box awaiting trial, his dreams disrupted, and his reputation under siege, after finding inspiration to take a stand for justice -all thanks to the resilient icon he passionately supports: Imran Khan.

Shah reflects: "My journey from promising business leader to 'terrorist' suspect started with a protest -responding from conscience as Khan was arrested on fabricated charges last May." He risked stigma and backlash to publicly back populist reformer Khan's ouster as prime minister this spring. Now enduring criminal prosecution and financial ruin, Shah draws resilience from his defiant role model, turfed from power after efforts to increase government accountability.

Shah's ideological alignment with Khan traces back years earlier to the former cricket legend's rise as an anti-corruption reformist. Khan inspired Shah's yearnings for principled governance as he built his business. "I admired Khan's vision for accountability and meritocracy lifting Pakistan to realise potential squandered by entitled dynasties lining pockets for decades. We craved institutions serving citizens, not interests of callous ruling class."

Yet Khan's dramatic PM dismissal shocked Shah's system as it did millions of distressed supporters. "That night, I joined swelling protests demanding fresh elections. Seeing Khan fight back from his hospital bed after being shot revitalised my activism -risk was justified, with democracy itself under siege."

In impassioned remarks at rallies, Shah slammed the new administration as illegally installed by foreign meddlers. He live-streamed confrontations with hostile police and rival loyalists. Then came an ominous signal of darker forces at play.

That week, authorities detained a college student employee of Shah's during small-scale civil disobedience. Shah explains his fateful choice: "Despite warnings, I felt compelled to ensure the safety of someone serving my company braving frontlines - so I rushed down, hoping my credentials as ex-parliament official would help secure the youth's release."

Instead, Shah found himself forcibly arrested as well --

stripped of the rights, protections, and power he previously moved within. The accompanying footage Shah captured went viral nationwide.

"My desperate pleas echoing uselessly against cold concrete walls symbolised the common man's subjugation by hostile state," Shah reflectively narrates.

The video concludes with Shah being tossed into the shadows. He would not re-emerge for two weeks.

Shah pauses, gazing towards a shaft of sunlight outside the courtroom, escaping between bars masking tall windows. The imposing space carries ghosts of the inhumane imprisonment that had nearly broken Shah's spirit months before, while awaiting his hearing.

"In police detention, I endured horrors --beaten, starved, stuffed inside stifling cells with actual terrorists for demanding basic rights." Scenes of the ordeal still torment his sleep. But Shah pushes through painful memories to detail the worst abuse. "A vicious commanding officer punched and kicked me without warning, ripping my last good shirt to shreds. His blows emphasised metallic threats to pile on charges if I kept resisting. Cruel laughter from other guards echoed through dark, sweat-lined halls whenever I pleaded for basic decency, my voice growing weaker from screaming names of family members I feared would never locate me..."

Shah's eyes fall with the shame of the memory. But fire returns quickly to his voice. "I refused to let evil men rob my dignity without a fight! So, from a battered floor, I proclaimed loyalty to my leader, Imran Khan. I knew his own suffering far exceeded mine."

Recalling Khan's principled example helped Shah survive the weeks deprived of a lawyer, or family knowledge of his whereabouts. But Shah's release delivered an unexpected emotional lift.

"I'll never forget my brave sister's first call to me from Saudi after my release, her voice projecting fierce pride instead of pity. This warrior woman made me lift my weary eyes through tears, still wearing tattered detention rags, as her consoling words reached across great distance to shelter my spirit," Shah shares.

Even their traditionalist mother stepped forward, embracing her son with praise for representing their family values, braving harm. "She declared no terrorist label could touch the man she raised, kneeling in grateful prayer -- liberating tears joined mine, streaming down her face."

These potent moments profoundly strengthened Shah's commitment to Khan's movement through further trials ahead. "My loved ones' courage inspired mine. I knew I could withstand anything by keeping loyal focus on my leader."

But police continued escalating pressure on Shah's dissent. A euphoric Independence Day rally led to another arrest --this time for the charge of displaying PTI insignia during celebrations. Shah shares: "My friend, Dr. Himayat, was arrested along with me that August 14th night just for the 'crime' of carrying a PTI flag. Shackled while waving Pakistan's flag, the absurd contrast fuelled citizens' outrage.

"When the additional SHO called my father about detaining me, he accused me of holding an Afghanistan flag -- absolutely false! My father affirmed I would carry a PTI or Pakistan flag, but never anything else."

An officer struck Shah for daring to question whether party representation made him a criminal. "That visceral public humiliation stirred anger against all who would degrade fellow citizens merely for political stances," he laments.

Authorities doubled down on leverage over the now-notorious figure. "Police commanders offered me a deal:-shift focus back to business empire and quit associating with Imran Khan, and they would drop charges. I directly rejected them -- 'No price can be put on principles!'"

The emotional and financial costs indeed rapidly mount

against the formerly thriving contractor. Onerous legal fees bleed Shah's resources, as delayed hearings require his repeated appearance. "The broken system presses endless, pointless proceedings, without even bothering to submit incriminating evidence against me! Such callous inefficiency sinks citizens deeper into suffering while the powerful escape all accountability."

Yet each weary mile travelled to sterile courtrooms and back marks another small victory of resistant spirit for Shah. "After withstanding the depths of their dungeons, fabricated allegations no longer carry weight to crush my soul!" Today, the state apparatus' full pressure sits deployed against Shah for his defiant loyalty to Imran Khan. No threats or deprivation at the ruthless hands of police and prosecutors prove enough to sever the tie.

"My leader, Imran Khan, stands resilient, forcing prospects of true people's democracy in Pakistan against all malicious efforts to silence his movement!" Shah passionately affirms.

"Seeing Khan withstand imprisonment and violence with conscience clean gives me strength through my smaller struggles --to represent all who demand their voice and vote be respected."

Shah glanced again towards the sole ray piercing through the courtroom's familiar, gloomy setting. "My trials will pass. But loyalty persists to reformist leaders like Khan, fighting for freedoms that uplift our nation against greedy individuals bent on keeping power through division and fear."

Syed Hamza Shah now calmly awaits the court's next actions as light fades from the expansive chamber. The young businessman understands his tribulation captures a nation's heightened tensions at this crossroads. But inside, Shah rests assured his struggle already marks monumental impact -- galvanising fellow citizens through a resonant example of courage, strengthening Pakistan's trajectory, favouring visionaries like Khan.

One day, the temporarily broken entrepreneur knows he will walk freely down bustling boulevards outside this courtroom. When citizens stop to greet the familiar visage from screens nationwide, they will recall an inspiring profile in stubborn resilience against injustice. And Shah hopes his steadfast loyalty towards Khan against all odds will remind Pakistanis of the potent power within people peacefully demonstrating for democratic reforms.

Shah concludes with a knowing smile both content and defiant: "Through my small story, now woven into Khan's greater stand for freedom, the roots of positive change dig deeper into new generations. Our intertwined legacies will bear the fruits of a society responsive to all citizens' voices."

Recalling the pivotal 2018 elections first bringing Khan to power, Shah shares his firm belief in the democratic power of voting over violence: "Despite suffering a terrible spine fracture in an accident, I still refuse to stand down --no injury could deter me from supporting momentous change. With my father's assistance, I proudly cast my ballot on crutches alongside fellow PTI supporters."

Shah affirms that he and Khan's followers shun extremism, instead championing elections as the only legitimate path to power. "We solely believe in using our democratic rights to vote and speak. I urge citizens:-take revenge for all state barbarity by turning out for reformists at the polls!"

7

"TO THE YOUTH I SAY, YOU ARE THE LEADERS OF TOMORROW. BELIEVE IN YOURSELF AND CHANGE THE WORLD FOR THE BETTER."

BELIEF IN YOUTH

My youth was undoubtedly the most defining time of my life. It was an era filled with fiery passion, boundless energy, and daring fearlessness. I took risks and jumped into challenges that I would likely shy away from today. Youth is truly a magical time, where you feel invincible and believe anything is possible.

In my late teens and twenties, I was fuelled by intense passion. I fiercely pursued my interests, whether it was travelling across the country or immersing myself in English literature. My mind was constantly abuzz with new ideas and big dreams. I would spend sleepless nights working on projects, too excited to rest. The passion that burned within led me to accomplish things I had never thought possible.

Along with passion came fearlessness. As a young woman, I challenged patriarchal norms by learning to cycle with my father, despite it being frowned upon. I was bold enough to study English literature at university, going against my community's belief that it wasn't useful for a girl. The thought of failing or disappointing my elders didn't hold me back. This audacity allowed me to step out of my comfort zone repeatedly.

I tried new hobbies, spoke up for causes I believed in, travelled alone -all without hesitation.

Looking back, this daring attitude was crucial to my growth. It enabled me to gain confidence and test my abilities. Had I been consumed by fear, I would have missed out on invaluable life lessons. I learned to pick myself up after falling, adapt when plans changed, and keep trying until I got it right. The courage to take risks and make mistakes transformed me.

Now in my late thirties, I am wiser, and my passions are oriented towards family. I think carefully before acting, and have a measured approach. While maturity brings prudence, I do miss the spiritedness of my youth. I could use some of that pluck now, when I am faced with tough decisions. While I may not make impulsive choices today, the resourcefulness I developed back then guides me. My youth gave me resilience and an unbreakable spirit.

Leaders across the world have long recognised the potential of young people. From Alexander the Great, who conquered the world in his twenties, to young revolutionaries like Bhagat Singh, who fought for India's independence,-history is full of young leaders and activists. Visionaries like Swami Vivekananda, Steve Jobs, and Mark Zuckerberg, made their mark when they were in their early twenties. Their drive to innovate changed the world.

In recent decades, there has been a conscious global effort to empower youth by including them in decision making. In 1995, the UN adopted World Programme of Action for Youth to increase opportunities for youth development. In 1999, Kofi Annan identified youth as agents of change and called for their social, economic, and political participation. The UN Security Council Resolution 2250, in 2015, called on nations to give youth a say in conflict resolution, counter-violence, and the promotion of peace.

Many world leaders today are ensuring youth have a seat at

the table. Jacinda Ardern, former prime minister of New Zealand, set up a Youth Advisory Group to advise her government on policies concerning young people. Canadian prime minister, Justin Trudeau, inducted a youth minister to represent youth interests in the Cabinet.

By engaging youth in governance, these leaders are not only securing the future but also gaining fresh perspectives. The idealism of young people pushes innovation. Their energy and technological fluency drives progress. By channelling youth power, visionary leadership ensures that this potential is not wasted. Giving young people agency and voice is our best hope for solving global challenges like climate change, poverty, and disease. Youth are not just the leaders of tomorrow, but the problem solvers of today. An empowered global youth community that works together across borders can save the planet.

As I enter the twilight of my life, I feel optimistic when I see vibrant young leaders advocating for change worldwide. The teenaged climate champion, Greta Thunberg, and the teenage gun reform activist, Emma Gonzalez, are shining examples. Through their conviction and courage, we can build a just world. The future rests in young hands.

My father would say that while he may never reclaim the passion and fearlessness of his own youth, he could nurture those qualities in me. By supporting me in my youth, he kept the spirit of young idealism alive and passed the torch to me. My father said his own youth made him who he was. By passing the torch to me, the next generation, he lit the spark in me that led to my self-discovery. Now, as a mother myself, I strive to do the same --nurture passion and fearlessness in my own children and pass on the torch to them. With thanks to my father and prayers for myself, I hope to successfully guide my children to blossom and carry forward the spirit of youth. We must celebrate the promise of youth and clear the path for them to bloom.

My leader, Imran Khan, is widely known for his tremendous focus and faith in the potential of the country's youth. Even as Khan enjoys widespread support from all age groups, his messaging and vision have consistently centred around energising and empowering the younger generation.

Right from PTI's early days, young people have formed the backbone of the party. Khan organised youth committees, campus chapters, and empowered young activists. He understood their passion for idealism, justice and healthier politics. Through direct outreach, he connected with youth concerns about transparency, meritocracy, better education, and employment. By giving them leadership roles, he groomed a new generation of politically conscious youth invested in national progress.

When Khan became prime minister in 2018, he appointed some younger ministers and advisors in an effort to include fresh perspectives; close to 25% of his cabinet were under 35 years old. This inclusion of fresh young talent was a clear signal of his trust and high expectations from youth. It shook up traditional power centres and gave young Pakistanis a greater stake in governance. Meritocracy was emphasised through initiatives like the Kamyab Jawan Programme to support youth entrepreneurship and skill training. The government has also made higher education a priority, including the provision of scholarships to increase enrollment.

In his speeches, Khan consistently addresses and encourages the youth. He reminds them that they are the future and must equip themselves with knowledge, empathy, justice, and perseverance. He says Pakistan will only change when its youth start believing in themselves and stand firm for truth like leaders such as Quaid-e-Azam. Khan's praise and trust has ignited young people's self-belief and patriotism.

They feel valued in national affairs, versus being sidelined earlier.

Beyond speeches, Khan promotes youth causes through action. The Sehat Insaf Card providing health insurance to all was enacted to support youth mobility and safety nets. Stipends and tuition assistance make education accessible. Digital skills training readies youth for modern opportunities. By listening to youth voices and including their perspective in policy, Khan has energized them to drive change.

My leader's focus on youth is not limited to Pakistanis. He takes his message globally by addressing youth in international forums. Khan asks privileged youth worldwide to support equity. He motivates young climate activists in the west to keep raising awareness. During the pandemic crisis, he called upon global youth leaders to join hands in tackling the health and economic challenges faced by the marginalised.

Imran Khan believes that an injustice anywhere is a threat to justice everywhere. His progressive international outlook resonates with liberal youth worldwide, while also appealing to conservative youth at home. By combining local socio-cultural relevance with universal human ideals, Khan has carved an unique place in young hearts. They see him as a reformist statesman, working for their futures rather than just political expediency.

While Khan's visionary leadership has inspired youth, support for him cuts across all demographic groups. The welfare policies mentioned earlier benefit families of all generations. Elders relate to his pious conduct and dislike of corruption. His world-class cricketing achievements make him a national hero and role model. By judiciously balancing Islamic values with modern aspirations, Khan has won trust across the generations and across various income groups.

Even critics acknowledge Khan's mass appeal and his ability to mobilise crowds. His impassioned oratory sparks people's emotions. The PTI's historic 2018 election victory was propelled by ardent youth activism as well as votes from older Pakistanis weary of misgovernance. Khan represents hope for a 'Naya Pakistan' free of dynastic politics, inequality, and corruption. This aspirational vision resonates strongly across age groups, even if the youth feel the most vigorously connected.

In a country where 60 percent of the population is under 30, Imran Khan has tapped into a powerful demographic force by making youth inclusion central to his governance philosophy. He knows that the energy and idealism of youth is Pakistan's biggest transformative force. Combined with the wisdom of elders, their collective strength can lift the nation to unprecedented development. Pakistan today sees vigorous youth participation in fields such as media, sports, arts, and community service. An entrepreneurship boom is underway. This reflects Khan's success in nurturing young talent.

To sum up, Imran Khan's magnetic persona and reformist agenda first catalysed the youth to rally behind him. Despite being jailed, Khan continues to inspire youth who stand steadfastly with him, even as the system works against him. By catalysing the power of youth, he has set Pakistan on the path to egalitarian growth. A major source of his widespread popularity among the youth are his passionate social media teams, or SMTs. These groups, comprising thousands of young volunteers, voice support for Khan on various platforms, like Twitter and Facebook. They relentlessly further his message and agenda without any monetary compensation. Their tireless dedication stems purely from belief in Imran Khan's vision. These social media teams have been instrumental in consolidating his robust youth support base. Their voluntary commitment highlights the depth of goodwill and loyalty Imran Khan enjoys among Pakistan's digitally engaged demographic.

We must acknowledge and thank these proactive young

advocates who provide the foundation for Khan's political rise. The world stands to gain from the coming of age of Pakistan's empowered youth demographic under Imran Khan's able leadership. With his unflagging spirit, the future is bright for the nation. One such youth is Zahid Danish, from Khyber Pakhtunkhwa, Pakistan.

Zahid Danish's dedication to PTI's cause began in 2009, as a- tenth-grade student galvanised by Imran Khan's vision. Hailing from the strictly Taliban-controlled Bannu district, the young Zahid defiantly took to the streets to promote his leader's message, despite initial ridicule --the start of a resilient 15-year journey of courageous activism marked by the odds stacked against this movement.

While studying from 2011-2014 at Islamia College, under future PTI minister Murad Saeed's mentorship, Zahid mobilised 25 youth volunteers, while narrowly surviving threats and a car accident returning from a PTI rally. His fortitude was witnessed on campus as Zahid took exams wheelchair-bound, earning his degree through sheer perseverance.

After graduating, Zahid devoted himself fully to PTI's ideals. He spent 27 days marching on the pivotal 2014 Islamabad standoff. Soon rising up the party ranks to head Bannu's youth wing, he has closely seen Imran Khan himself and has worked along with the entire PTI senior leadership over momentous years for Pakistan's future.

This allegiance was tested when opposing parties dangled bribes of up to two crore rupees in 2021 for Zahid to abandon PTI --offers swiftly rejected by this loyalist, named as heir to a family legacy once aligned to ANP party interests.

Yet the backlash only intensified after Imran Khan's controversial 2022 ouster. Already scarred from previous Taliban threats, Zahid now bears the weight of three separate FIR cases brought upon him along with new messages from shady quarters to cease his activism altogether. But this 30-

year-old sub-engineer and former professor remains undeterred.

To Zahid Danish, Imran Khan's "Haqiqi Azadi" vision symbolises the last stand for justice in a system stacked towards oppression and corruption. No matter what, this soldier vows to stand by his leader "till the last drop of blood" --his story now eternally intertwined with Pakistan's future.

While Zahid Danish's name will be etched into PTI lore for his fearless loyalty since age 15, his story also epitomises the pro-Imran Khan fervour sweeping Pakistan's youth demographics. As someone raised under strict Taliban influence in Bannu, Zahid overcame community barriers, alongside evolving personal family politics, to become a diehard Khan supporter. This journey symbolically mirrors that of millions of passionate youth rallied in solidarity behind Imran Khan's bold vision for Pakistan's future. They see a rare combination of strengths: bravery against demonstrably compromised opposition forces, strength to persevere through persistent obstacles, and sincerity in not yielding to temptation as power can corrupt. This grassroots tsunami of youth loyalty stems from identifying their own frustrated aspirations with an incorruptible determined change-maker. Under Imran's defiant example, daring to directly confront longstanding tyrannical structures, the Pakistani youth finally feels represented by a credible voice, speaking and fighting for their future against all odds. Just like their leader, this generation will fearlessly pursue his "Haqiqi Azadi" mission till their last breaths if they have to.

The sparks of defiance among Pakistan's youth towards corrupt governance first flashed at NUST University, where the caretaker PM's tardy arrival was openly challenged as symbolic of politicians' self-serving attitudes that rob the public's time and trust. This audacious tone continued in questioning the premier's commitment to accountability amid pressure to whitewash the former regime's abuses of authority. In that ironically symbolic first act, Pakistan's caretaker PM's late arrival exposed an audience already simmering with frustration towards the political status quo. The premier NUST University venue quickly transformed into an impromptu public interrogation, not sparing any punches.

One young woman put the premier bluntly on the spot, asking why he deemed his time more valuable by keeping thousands of energetic youth waiting. Loud cheers interjected before he could respond to the audacious direct call-out. Undeterred, she smoothly transitioned to drill corruption failures she blamed as the cause of Pakistan's current vulnerability and loss of rights. This bold line of questioning set the tone.

Another young man targeted investigatory inconsistencies seemingly protecting embedded political perpetrators, despite obvious breaches of trust and national plunder. Each evasive response from the platform drew waves of mocking dissent from the riled-up youths.

The explosive exchanges signified the last vestiges of Pakistan's culture of blind hierarchical obedience fading in lieu of youth seizing their voice. This generation will openly challenge even the highest offices without reservation regarding uncomfortable truths. Their numbers and unity behind figures like Imran Khan, who are brave enough to take on entrenched abusive powers, foreshadow a new democratic order aligning to the common man's interests instead of the elite's.

The aggression escalated shortly after, at the 2023 Capital Youth Expo, where powerful representatives from Pakistan's media and security establishments faced a verbal lashing. Veteran journalist Talat Hussain was lambasted for seeming to protect ex-leaders by peddling alleged propaganda instead of hard-hitting facts. The confrontation turned even more explosive when students asked about the military's inability to provide state protection to national hero, Dr. Abdul Qadeer Khan. Youth anger also indirectly boiled over regarding the establishments' failure to safeguard Imran Khan against implicit threats seeking to deter his anti-corruption crusade.

This wave of brazen public criticism directed towards the highest offices in Pakistan reflects the nation's youth finding their voice as a formidable check against traditional centres of unchecked power. Having borne the brunt of corruption and instability, their numbers, armed behind uncompromising truth-tellers like Imran Khan, will steward the moral realignment to build an equitable democracy that respects civil rights. With this awakened generation unafraid to speak openly against abuse and misconduct, the future of integrity in public service looks brighter in Pakistan.

8

"THERE ARE GREATER GOALS IN LIFE THAN MATERIAL AND SENSUAL PLEASURES"

LIVING WITH PURPOSE

In today's world, dominated by consumerism and instant gratification, it is easy to get caught up in the pursuit of material possessions and sensual enjoyments. Luxury items, lavish vacations, cars, gadgets --these tangible things promise to make our lives easier, more comfortable, and full of pleasure. However, focusing solely on acquiring wealth, objects, and indulging the senses can often leave one feeling unfulfilled. There are greater goals in life that bring deeper rewards.

Contributing to something beyond oneself gives meaning and purpose. Whether it is through raising children, volunteering for a cause or dedicating oneself to a vocation, being part of something bigger provides a sense of fulfilment that cannot be matched by material pleasures. Investing time and effort to make a positive impact on the community and environment also brings immense satisfaction.

Developing the self is a worthy pursuit. Learning new skills, expanding one's mind through reading and study, travelling to gain new perspective -these activities lead to personal growth. Intellectual and spiritual development is extremely enriching and helps us actualise our human potential. Cultivating strong relationships based on empathy and compassion is among the most noble goals. Nurturing bonds of affection and care with family, friends, partners and others is deeply fulfilling. The happiness we find in such selfless connections cannot be substituted by any possessions. Living with integrity and working for causes like justice, equality and human rights can be very rewarding, even if material benefits are small. The peace and contentment that comes from righteous living is a treasure. Leaving the world a little better than we found it is an admirable aspiration.

While a certain level of financial security and comfort is essential, getting caught in a mindless rat race for more luxury and pleasure can leave us restless. Moderation and balance are key. The greatest happiness comes from having larger goals based on self-realisation, contribution to others, and working for things beyond our selfish interests. True contentment lies within, not in fleeting sensory enjoyments. Keeping this perspective allows us to live a deeply meaningful life.

Throughout history, the most impactful leaders have been those who lived meaningfully in pursuit of higher ideals. They stood out by leading lives centred around spiritual development, service to humanity, and contributing to the greater good. Prophet Muhammad (PBUH), other prophets, Allama Iqbal, Quaid-e-Azam, and leaders like Imran Khan offer shining examples of surrendering worldly temptations to fulfill a greater purpose.

Prophet Muhammad's (PBUH) life was the epitome of virtuous living. As Islam's final messenger, his mission was to spread the message of monotheism, kindness, justice and spiritual devotion in the world. All his efforts were wholly dedicated to fulfilling this role as God's messenger and leading by example. He gave up a comfortable merchant life to take on the hardships of prophethood and spent all his time serving humanity.

Even when he triumphed over enemies, Prophet Muhammad (PBUH) lived simply, wore coarse clothing and ate humble food. He sought no thrones or riches but lived akin to the poorest in his community. His marriages after the death of his first wife, Khadija, were primarily contracted to support widowed or divorced women, when very few options existed for lone women. He endured immense grief with the deaths of many children. Through loss and hardship, he persevered in his mission.

Prophet Muhammad's (PBUH) character was governed wholly by spiritual ideals like generosity, courage, forgiveness and honesty. His compassion and benevolence as God's messenger impacted millions across centuries. By surrendering material comforts and sensual desires, he attained spiritual fulfilment and eternal renown.

Other prophets like Isa, Musa, Ibrahim, and Nuh, (AS) too, devoted their lives to spreading God's message and guiding people to righteousness. They patiently endured mockery and persecution from disbelievers. They led lives marked by prayer, charity, and detachment from wealth. Through Divine Calling, these prophets found meaning by turning away from worldly pleasures and fully committing to their higher purpose.

Pakistan's national poet, Allama Iqbal, lived a deeply spiritual and intellectual life, guided by a philosophy of self-development and the revival of Islamic civilisation. As an academic and scholar, his lifelong pursuit of knowledge and cultivation of wisdom left a lasting legacy in the form of his poetry and prose.

Iqbal studied extensively in Europe, where he was exposed to modern philosophy and western modes of thought. But he resolutely clung to spiritual growth and an eastern outlook on life. He travelled widely to gain perspective but chose to live simply. Material riches held no significance for him compared to enriching his mind. His non-conformist ideas were unconstrained by pursuit of power, fame or wealth.

Iqbal called for spiritual awakening through his works while criticising materialism. His vision for revived Islamic society was rooted in ideals of justice and human dignity over worldly dogmas. By devoting his life to knowledge and advocating lofty principles, Iqbal secured an immortal place in history.

As father of the nation, Quaid-e-Azam Mohammad Ali Jinnah's performed one of the greatest services for humanity by securing freedom for Muslims of the subcontinent. This achievement required tremendous personal sacrifice and single-minded devotion.

For much of his life as a lawyer and congress leader, Jinnah was at the peak of affluence and influence. However, in his later years, he left behind his lucrative practice and elite social circles to assume leadership of the Muslim League. Faced with failing health and implacable opposition, he persevered tirelessly towards the goal of an independent Pakistan.

Jinnah forged Muslim unity and mobilised millions with his force of will and the power of his principles. He rearranged his private life to accommodate his public mission, even enduring the heartbreak of separation from his beloved daughter, Dina. Jinnah's conduct was governed by integrity, discipline, and total commitment to the Cause till his last breath.

The austerity and gravity with which Jinnah led during the Pakistan Movement, as well as his brief tenure as Governor General, set the standard for selfless service. His life, much like that of the founding fathers of religion and nations before him, was devoted to fulfilling the destiny of his people, rather than personal glory.

Like his towering predecessors, Imran Khan is another leader who has won worldwide admiration by living with purpose and eschewing material temptations. During his spectacular sports career, Imran Khan attained immense fame and fortune as Pakistan's most successful cricket captain. However, he left behind cricket at the peak of his sporting career and invested his time and earnings in building Pakistan's first cancer hospital. For over two decades, he tirelessly collected funds and oversaw the hospital's construction and operations. His dedication to helping cancer patients marked the beginning of his second innings in public service.

Before entering politics, Imran Khan enjoyed an affluent lifestyle as a cricket legend and philanthropist. But he gave up his peaceful existence to challenge the corrupt ruling class through the Pakistan Tehree-e-Insaf party. For many years, he endured mockery and hopelessness as a 'one-man squad' against the political elite. His successful political struggle was fuelled by the passion for reforming the country along meritocratic lines. Victory for Imran Khan was never about assuming power and authority. It was about establishing the rule of law and accountability, providing social welfare and reforming governance -goals greater than any personal ambition.

During his tenure as prime minister, Imran Khan has adopted a simple lifestyle free of ostentation. He inhabits a modest home instead of the prime minister's palatial house. He auctions lavish state gifts and uses the proceeds for humanitarian causes. Imran Khan's vision, policies and conduct all aim to lift Pakistan out of corruption towards national regeneration.

As a famous sportsman and later political leader, Imran Khan's public life has often been maligned by opponents levying false allegations like drug addiction. However, none of their smear campaigns have succeeded in tarnishing Imran Khan's character. Recent medical reports during his unjust imprisonment clearly reveal no substance abuse. After over three months in jail, comprehensive blood tests found absolutely no trace of narcotics.

In fact, Imran Khan maintains his physical fitness even in jail by performing basic exercises, as per his legal right. His legal team has been compelled to repeatedly demand proper permission for his workouts, contradicting claims that he depends on drugs or reckless living. At age 71, his commitment to health and discipline clearly dispels all malicious propaganda. Imran Khan draws his strength not from addictive substances, but from his lifelong crusade for justice. His enemies have failed time and again to deter this struggle through character assassination. Imran Khan's honourable conduct continues to frustrate their nefarious designs.

The highest evolved leaders across time prioritised spiritual enrichment, intellectual growth, and service to humanity over chasing material pleasures. Lofty goals fuelled their lives. By renouncing the pull of power and wealth in favour of pursuing higher ideals, they optimised their human experience. Living purposefully sometimes required immense courage and sacrifice, but the fulfilment was far greater. The presence of family and cherished relationships added meaning, but were not sole objectives. Intentness on their vision liberated these leaders from egoistic impulses and petty distractions. High-mindedness fuelled their days. Such extraordinary resolve seems almost impossible in the age of instant gratification, where self-discipline is scarce. But history bears testament that those who deny shallow desires are granted richer insights. They appeal to our deepest aspirations. Their lives serve as timeless inspiration and a reminder that there are goals far greater than the mundane.

My late father had always believed in living for a higher purpose. Despite challenges, he was determined to break from tradition and enable his children to be educated. When his own brothers and sisters led lives without formal education, or any interest in sending their children to school, my father charted a different path. He endured ridicule and hardship to send me and my siblings to school, believing deeply in education's transformative power.

Today, all the academic degrees I hold are thanks to my father's foresight and sacrifice. He transformed not just his own children's lives but uplifted our entire family. The fact that I am even in a position to write this book is a direct result of his efforts. Though my beloved father is no longer in this world to see the fruits of his labour, I know he must be looking down happily from heaven. By pursuing knowledge, his labour enabling education, he lived a life of great purpose. I strive to fulfil his noble aspirations through my work. In brilliant contrast to the status quo of corruption and excess, Imran Khan exhorts his loyal supporters towards purpose and meaning beyond shallow sensual pleasures --and they ardently follow his lead with great fervour. Khan has established supremely high expectations for the quality of life's work, thought, and moral purpose amongst his devoted followers. Inspired profoundly by their venerable leader, PTI loyalists live courageously with integrity, willing to sacrifice comforts and confront fears so they may strive nobly towards national freedom and righteousness. Khan's uncompromising standards demand of his admirers discipline and bravery, of which they are asked to give their utmost. Thus, those choosing to truly walk in Imran Khan's footsteps traverse a path of fearless sacrifice, living not for decadent short-term gratification but for purpose and principle tied to the prosperity of Pakistan and its people. The PTI faithful subsume and transcend personal goals, transformed by the higher calling of service embodied by their captain --Imran Khan.

Raoof Hasan, the former Special Assistant to ex-PM Imran Khan, commented in an X-Space on the public show of support for Khan at the 10 December motor cycle rally in Lahore, stating: "As Imran Khan says, the people of Pakistan have 'broken the fear barrier' and the large turnout for the PTI convention is conspicuously clear evidence that the people overwhelmingly want Imran Khan back."

When one participant asked how the public can support Khan, saying "The public needs only Imran Khan," Raoof replied: "We all wish to free Khan, but we are in a country where there are no institutions, there is no democracy --just a few people seeking to demolish PTI and our leader."

He added optimistically: "But after darkness, there is always light. We are engaged in a legal battle and with peaceful education, we look forward to getting Pakistan freed sooner rather than later."

On Khan's return, Raoof stated: "Imran Khan will soon be among us all and will be working for Pakistan's progress in an even better way than before."

While painting a dire picture of Pakistan's current institutional failings, Raoof expressed confidence in both the widespread public support for Imran Khan, as evidenced in the 10 December rally turnout, and Khan's imminent return to leadership after the party navigates its legal challenges. He reaffirmed the party's commitment to peaceful political engagement. Speaking confidently about the PTI's growing strength, Raoof stated: "With every passing day, our party is getting stronger and our conventions are being held all around the country. The flames of support are getting higher."

He predicted the movement's future growth, saying: "Sooner, PTI workers' conventions will be held all around the world and people will join us from everywhere."

On the subject of elections, Raoof suggested the state is afraid of Imran Khan's popularity, stating: "If there's an election on 8th Feb 2024, the state would run away from the election until they're sure PTI will be defeated. In my personal view, they're afraid to conduct elections."

Describing alleged state obstruction efforts, he continued: "The state is engaged in different conspiracies to restrict observers and journalists from monitoring the election."

Raoof expressed supreme confidence in the surging public support for PTI, as evidenced in their convention turnouts; predicted the movement's global growth; and believes the state machinations indicate a fear of Imran Khan's popularity among voters --hence their avoidance of free and fair elections PTI is poised to win. He implies unfair and opaque election engineering efforts are underway.

Raoof's staunchly optimistic statements regarding the monumental turnouts at recent PTI conventions highlight the brimming enthusiasm of the Pakistani public to vocally and fearlessly stand in support of Khan. Clearly evidenced by the impressive, swelling crowds at PTI gatherings, first in Khyber Pakhtunkhwa, and now massively in Punjab, Khan continues to draw tens of thousands of passionate, flag-waving supporters chanting pro-Khan slogans. This towering public display of solidarity for the ousted PM, defiantly backing Khan in the face of the state's authoritarian crackdowns and arrests, demonstrates the common people's burning desire for his return and refusal to be intimidated into silence. The cascading crowds, essentially bursting at the seams during PTI conventions, indicate Khan's widespread popularity remains undeniably strong amongst the Pakistani people, while openly flouting the state's brutal efforts to disrupt, diminish and dismantle the PTI movement.

Raoof highlights the crumbled barrier of fear amongst Khan's followers as they fill convention venues beyond maximum capacity, braving police threats and state repression through their unified show of support for Imran Khan's vision.

Though the shadowy state machinations continue, the PTI's conventions clearly exhibit an unassailable popular backing amongst the masses. This growing groundswell, evidenced by the conventions' sheer scale and passion, fuels anticipation of a PTI sweep when free and fair elections are finally held.

This sweeping show of support is also evident across social media platforms, which are replete with emotional videos posted by Khan's ardent followers across Pakistan and the world.

These videos feature people passionately proclaiming their trust in Khan, not just as the destined leader of the Pakistani nation, but of the entire Muslim ummah worldwide. With tears in their eyes, and fists pumped in solidarity, Khan's supporters in these viral clips declare they stand firmly behind him because they believe Allah has chosen him to unite and lead Muslims globally towards justice and progress.

From the streets to the screens, the outpouring of support from all corners—from Pakistani villagers to Gulf businessmen —shows Khan has become a transcendent figure who many trust deeply to represent and champion their causes. This expansive digital platform enables a broader demonstration of the unmatched popular backing Khan enjoys across Pakistan and beyond its borders.

The sheer passion evidenced in these videos adds further credence to Raoof's statements about the crumbled barrier of fear amongst Khan's swelling follower base. Despite authoritarian crackdowns, they continue harnessing social platforms to openly declare their single-minded support for Khan's visionary leadership of marginalised Muslim populations across the world.

9

"TO EMPOWER WOMEN IS TO DEVELOP A NATION."

PROMOTING GENDER EQUALITY AND SUPPORTING WOMEN

As a woman myself, with a mother, sisters, and many wonderful women who have touched my life, I firmly believe that life simply would not be possible without the contributions of women. This belief does not stem merely from my convictions but has foundations in religious scriptures, history, and reason.

Both the Quran and the Bible illustrate how instrumental women are in furthering mankind. The creation story in both holy books speaks of how Adam needed Eve in order to procreate and spawn future generations. This establishes how foundational women's reproductive capabilities are for a functioning society. Beyond childbirth, women play irreplaceable roles as mothers, nurturing each new person with immense care, patience and selflessness.

Expanding beyond motherhood, women enrich lives through all familial, friendly, professional, and community relationships. As sisters, wives, colleagues, friends,-women form the backbone of support, understanding, and human connectivity on which fulfilling lives rely. A world devoid of women would severely lack colour, vibrancy, empathy, and meaning.

My own mother, though frequently constrained by social conformity and convention, provided steadfast love and worked tirelessly to raise me and my siblings. Her risk-averse approach may have limited her personal growth at times, due to fear of societal disapproval, but she chose it to secure our wellbeing. As a non-conformist, I have made bolder choices, questioning norms which do not align with my morals,-but we both contribute social value in our unique ways. This speaks to how diverse women's approaches can be, yet all remain essential threads in the social fabric.

While male domination endures in political and corporate leadership, I believe history often obscures the full extent of remarkable women in decision-making roles. Historians reflecting broader misogyny have diminished accomplishments of powerful female leaders, thinkers, scientists, and change-makers. But the influence of such women throughout civilisation has undoubtedly pushed humanity forward, despite inequality.

When I examine admirable leaders like Imran Khan, I recognise that leadership potential often germinates within a nurturing family network cultivated by strong parenting partnerships --both mothers and fathers play crucial roles. While historically, child-rearing fell to women disproportionately, especially in older generations, the active involvement of fathers in their children's moral, emotional and intellectual development is equally instrumental for positive outcomes.

In Khan's case, while credit likely belongs more to his mother, based on gender norms of the time, his father was likely also integral in instilling the values that bolstered Khan's dedication to public service and unrelenting conviction. My views about Khan's mother's outsized influence stem from assumptions rooted in broader societal attitudes, which minimised paternal participation in past decades. His grief over her passing, and his decision to name the cancer hospital after her signifies her profound inspirational role, but his father likely also meaningfully shaped Khan's worldview and leadership abilities in ways less visible.

Moving forward, the most effective leadership development will stem from family units, wherein both mothers and fathers share parenting duties and pass on ethical underpinnings central to rearing engaged, empathetic and civically-driven children. Equitable participation of men and women in nurturing future change-makers can accelerate progress.

The support of Khan's sisters has also buoyed him during difficult political and social battles, when opposition falsely targeted his character. His sisters bravely stepped forward to defend Khan's integrity. Without their loyalty and counsel, Khan would undoubtedly have struggled more in persevering as a leader in the face of controversy.

This underscores my firm belief that male leaders who achieve lasting greatness are frequently bolstered by encouraging women --whether mothers, sisters, daughters, colleagues or friends. While misogyny has long downplayed such partnerships, men relying on skilful guidance from women is an oft-ignored historical reality.

One remarkable aspect of Imran Khan's leadership is galvanising an impassioned following among women across Pakistan, even those living under stringent patriarchal constraints. From uneducated women in rural villages to highly educated urban professionals, Khan's reform message resonates. Given cultural and religious barriers limiting women's civic participation, Khan has uniquely managed to attract substantial female support in his push for national change.

Both women and men comprise Khan's devotees willing to

withstand threats in backing his movement. During state crackdowns on Khan, female supporters defiantly stood vigil outside his home, despite shelling and brutal physical attacks on protestors. Even female prisoners have elicited Khan's concern and advocacy, underscoring his staunch support for women's welfare and equality.

These diehard female devotees, willing to bear the brunt of violence alongside male cadres, represent a noteworthy shift for women often prevented from actively participating in politics. By spurring them into the public sphere, at personal risk, Khan has mobilised a formidable force for reform.

This expansive female support refutes critics who misconstrue Khan's religious piety as fundamentalism. The visible activism and ownership demonstrated by his women supporters, regardless of education or ethnicity, proves Khan's inclusive development agenda resonates across demographics. From empowering women to access education and jobs, to elevating them as drivers of community development, Khan's vision for gender justice has mobilised women. They can envisage real progress through his emphasis on women-led initiatives for poverty alleviation and human development.

By boldly entering the political arena to back Khan's reform movement, Pakistani women display their conviction that he represents the best hope for a more equitable future. Their spirited voice and influence as a pressure group for change, with sacrifice equal to men's, will steer Pakistan's trajectory. With Khan amplifying female participation, their input will shape more representative and sustainable national policies.

Imran Khan's well-documented marriages provide insight into his staunch respect for women, despite intense public scrutiny. Across his three weddings, to Jemima Goldsmith, Reham Khan, and Bushra Bibi, Khan exercised discretion, even when facing defamatory remarks. His concern for his spouses' wellbeing and honour demonstrates a commitment to countering misogynistic attitudes.

Khan's first marriage, to Jemima Goldsmith, persisted across fierce cultural barriers and media glare. While some Islamic scholars denounced the Anglican-Pakistani union, Khan stood steadfast with Goldsmith, crediting her grace and work in launching Shaukat Khanum hospital. Even in divorce, he maintained affection and deflected gossip to protect her privacy.

His brief second marriage, to journalist Reham Khan, concluded quickly and cordially with minimal public disparagement afterwards. Despite Reham targeting Imran in a controversial memoir implying drug use and sexual impropriety, Khan refused counter-allegations. His restraint revealed maturity and resolve to avoid dishonourable personal attacks, irrespective of provocation.

Khan's current wife, Bushra Bibi, being central to his spiritual life, elicits overt protectiveness. During court proceedings against Khan, he is seen shielding Bibi from crowds, bespeaking his care for her wellbeing. Reports suggest that even in jail recently, Khan frequently enquired anxiously about Bibi's health, underscoring spousal devotion exceeding personal troubles.

This pattern of grace towards former partners and vigilant concern for current spouses is rare for prominent figures, especially politicians. Khan's pointed avoidance of airing grievances and his dedication to guarding wives from harm demonstrates progressive values of responsibility, fidelity, and integrity within relationships.

In a cultural landscape still battling patriarchy and often trivialising divorces or political marriages, Khan sets an example through discretion. By considering spousal dignity non-negotiable regardless of circumstance, he embodies a nobility too frequently lacking in public discourse about women linked to leaders.

Some critics argue Khan's marriages themselves demonstrate male entitlement and contradict his championing of women's rights. But relationships involve personal nuances between consenting partners. Beyond superficial perception, Khan's record shows no pattern of exploiting power dynamics. Instead, his genuine partnerships with independent, accomplished women reveal mutual fondness and parity.

With Jemima Goldsmith, there appeared no ulterior motive besides open-minded efforts at cross-cultural understanding. While the marriage ended, Goldsmith continues voicing support for Khan's leadership, suggesting no ill-treatment. Reham Khan's ambitiousness and subsequent book implies her agency rather than victimhood. And Bibi's spiritual guidance to Khan contradicts assumptions of coercion.

Each marriage, on analysis, seems to have positively impacted Khan's tolerance, empathy and respect for women. His refusal to malign former wives, uncommon in a political world rife with acrimonious separations, demonstrates evolution. This nuanced view aligns with Khan's broader advocacy of gender equity. If anything, his avoidance of misogynistic Muslim stereotypes --through partnerships with independent western women --increases the perception of sincerity when promoting women's welfare.

Some may understandably argue Khan's privileged position allowed multiple marriages, reflecting double-standards. But scrutinising individual conduct within cultural restraints is unproductive if institutional inequity remains unchanged. As leader, Khan's voluntary positive example can influence gradual attitude shifts towards relationships and wives -- especially regarding dignity and consent.

Ultimately, Khan's personal equation with wives seems

instructive for men struggling to balance religious orientations with modern demands of gender parity. That Khan remains drawn towards bold, career-driven women despite backlash, reveals an ability for self-reflection rather than clinging to outdated patriarchal models. His complementary regard for Bibi's spiritual mentorship further confirms an openness to feminine authority, surpassing paternalistic religious interpretations.

Through the compassionate way Khan conducts marital relationships --prioritising dignity irrespective of conditions — he provides a constructive playbook. His avoidance of vindictiveness when politically and socially convenient, proves wilful self-discipline. In a region needing to counter regressive attitudes that functionally constrain women despite legal progression, Khan's personal conduct promotes progressive possibilities. With national conditions primed for a renaissance, guided by restorative justice across all demographics, Khan's personal evolution hints at the reform he may spearhead on national scale.

Islam itself lays the foundation for women's liberation, independence and leadership since its advent. Examining the life of Prophet Muhammad (PBUH) reveals the heights of respect, dignity, and decision-making authority he conferred upon his wives and daughters. His partnerships with empowered women shattered norms in a society given to entrenched misogyny. By entrusting women as teachers of theology, jurisprudence, literacy and more, Prophet Muhammad (PBUH) established Islam as a human rights vanguard elevating female potential beyond seventh-century Arabia's attitudes.

The matrimonial contracts Prophet Muhammad (PBUH) organised stipulated independent wealth management rights for wives --an unprecedented legal provision in those times, securing financial autonomy for women. By ensuring they retained control over earnings and property, he empowered them to leave marriages at will without fearing destitution. This profound gesture centuries ahead of its time enabled wives like Khadijah bint Khuwaylid, an accomplished businesswoman, to retain professional independence alongside domesticity. By pointedly hiring disadvantaged women like former slave Zaynab bint Jahsh as clerks, he demonstratively valued their economic participation outside homes.

The Prophet moreover sought counsel from wives like Umm Salamah on diplomatic decisions and treaty negotiations. By incorporating wives within machinations of statehood otherwise reserved for male tribal elders, he displayed confidence in women's intellectual capacities as equals. Allowing their feedback to guide complicated mediations proved instrumental in unifying fractious groups into accepting his revolutionary leadership.

Through his parting sermon too, Prophet Muhammad (PBUH) explicitly directed followers to reform backwards cultural attitudes towards women by elevating their status as revered mothers in society. By emphasising that they bear and nurture coming generations, he highlighted women as instrumental to securing communal futures. Through bestowing wives and daughters like Fatima Zahra with utmost love and respect, despite opposition, Prophet Muhammad (PBUH) walked the talk on equitable relationships under divine benevolence --establishing the basis for Islamic worldviews to cherish femininity for centuries.

This profound blueprint for honouring women's space, voices, and rights within Arabia's prevailing toxicity helped Islamic leadership diverge sharply from contemporary misogyny across rival power structures. The needle moved from viewing women as insignificant property to invaluable partners in engendering social progress.

While pluralistic Islamic society saw occasional regressive periods, the transcendent example set by Prophet Muhammad

(PBUH) was frequently revived by forward-thinking scholars and rulers. As political successors expanded Muslim realms, notable leaders, like Caliph Umar Ibn Al-Khattab, appointed elite councils of eminent women to consult on social policies and legislation. Ottoman leadership positions, entrusted to prominent wives and daughters, underscored continual efforts at maximising female participation domestically and administratively.

This historical reality of Islam's revolutionary positioning of women in society, economy and governance sharply contrasts with cultures of patriarchy, marginalisation and exploitation manifesting across Islamic regions in recent centuries. The gulf between Islamic tenets and cultural practice on gender rights requires urgent redress.

As both national hero and Islamic idealist, my leader, Imran Khan, represents a rare leadership committed to resurrecting original Islamic principles on women's empowerment. Following Prophet Muhammad's (PBUH) Sunnah, Khan supports women's visibility and voices within political machinery long monopolised by men.

Like his national leader, Imran Khan, my father always empowered his wife as an equal decision-maker guiding our family's path. He considered her counsel indispensable, refusing any unilateral choices impacting household or child-rearing matters without her consent. His actions brought to life the reverential Islamic approach to matrimony within a milieu that typically restricted women to domestic duties devoid of authority.

Despite enduring mockery from his conservative Pashtun brothers regarding his deference to his wife, my father remained unapologetic about upholding her dignity as an empowered equal. He consciously rejected the patriarchal assumption of wives existing solely to serve husbands, children, and in-laws without reciprocity. By insisting his brothers acknowledge his wife's wishes, he complicated norms.

My mother consequently enjoyed rare autonomy in contributing her intellect and emotional intelligence to navigating critical moments. My father shielded her from conservative attempts to restrict her self-expression. She reciprocated this trust in her capabilities by taking co-ownership of financial decisions, parenting challenges, household administrative matters, and more. This partnership liberated my mother to pursue professionalism through reading Islamic history and women's magazines, with my father handling domestic responsibilities in her absence.

In effect, my parents' marriage manifested the Prophet Muhammad's (PBUH) vision of relationships built on mutual consultation rather than gendered hierarchy. My father's willingness to endure social sanctions in order to facilitate my mother's pursuit of reading books and magazines signalled his championship of women's rights. By using his male privilege to insist on her empowerment, he became her ally in a stifling milieu.

In leading through this personal example, my father provided me enduring lessons regarding respect across gender. His marriage remains my template for equitable associations between spouses, beyond power asymmetry. By mirroring the model established by Imran Khan, who considers wives like Bushra Bibi irreplaceable counsellors, my father illuminated an ideal Islamic partnership.

In emulating Prophet Muhammad's (PBUH) conduct, where wives actively contributed to shaping history, both Khan and my father planted seeds for a national rebirth. Their conviction in empowered women as co-creators of existence offers hope against cultures imbued in patriarchy. By living out Quranic principles of harmony between life partners, they invoke the heritage of Islam's revolutionary championship of women against repression.

Imran Khan's agenda for inclusive national development and democratic participation aims to uplift women marginalised by decades of kleptocracy and elitism presided over by dynastic political families. By actively spurring socioeconomic mobility for women through initiatives like interest-free microfinance loans, vocational skills training, entrepreneurial incubators and more, Khan, during his government, had sought to restore their status as equal partners. This commitment aligned with foundational Islamic principles regarding the honourable and equitable treatment of women.

Khan recognises that structural reforms enshrining women's welfare socially and economically are non-negotiable prerequisites for establishing an Islamic welfare state. Pakistan currently faces immense crises fuelled by runaway inflation, currency declines, floods, radicalisation and more --outcomes of long-term policies entrenching inequality, nepotism and oligarchy while ignoring majority interests. Khan understands that only by pursuing urgent reform, stamped by Quranic injunctions to uplift and empower women, as per Prophet Muhammad's (PBUH) own example, can the prevalent challenges be systematically overcome.

Ordinary Pakistani women have faced the worst marginalisation under regimes dominated by family dynasties which concentrate wealth and opportunity in few hands. By deliberately expanding women's access to education, finance, legal protections, skill-based employment and leadership opportunities, Khan aims to restore their status as equal partners, integral to national building. With women thus activated through his reforms to become growth catalysts, micro-enterprises to multinational corporations stand to gain productivity, essential for economic revival.

No doubt, female political prisoners like Sanam Javeed, Tayaba Raja and Khadija Shah display remarkable resilience and ideological commitment in continuing to stand with Imran Khan, despite intense pressure. Their refusal to compromise or disavow their support, despite being offered relief for compliance, is unprecedented in Pakistan's political landscape. Javeed's letters from prison to her family clearly articulate her unconditional backing for Khan's vision, regardless of personal cost. Other dissenters forced to denounce Khan in choreographed press conferences have secured release from charges. However, these women's staunch refusal to partake in political theatre for expedient freedom underscores rare conviction. Their steadfast loyalty, despite incarceration on likely fabricated grounds, proves Khan's ability to inspire ordinary citizens with his qualities of fearlessness, purpose and self-belief. Javeed, Raja and Shah embodied Khan's mantle of resistance against tyranny at great risk. Their brave incarceration has turned them into symbols of defiance against state excess.

Unlike opportunists swapping loyalty for liberty, these women represent the essence of principled politics --sticking to truth irrespective of coercion or intimidation. Their sacrifice throws into stark relief the bankrupt political culture of Pakistan thriving on patronage, pressure and persecution. With nothing personally to gain, these female prisoners give voice to Khan's vision for system change based on moral courage. Their plight has awakened citizens to the depths of establishment-led repression.

A salient feature of Khan's political career is empowering everyday citizens to access their own leadership potential in fuelling his reform agenda. Breaking elitist norms of treating voters as passive sheep, Khan actively nurtures capacities for civic participation across gender, ethnic and religious lines. His investment in grooming party workers to take ownership of processes has created a thriving grassroots ecosystem reflecting genuine democratic mobilisation. The courage witnessed among female prisoners, enduring oppression because of their belief in his vision, underscores this leadership transfer in motion.

Unlike figureheads hovering above cadres and restricting inner-party discourse, Khan's openness to ideas from below, and accessibility as leader encourages bigger goal internalisation. By patiently elevating ordinary citizens as partners through political education and trust instead of top-down command-control, Khan is organically expanding leadership to strengthen democratic roots. The promise of decentralised decision-making is manifesting through the responsible civic participation of women like Sanam Javeed, willing to accept incarceration to protect the mandate. Khan is effectively distributing his reform philosophy across sections, signalling more participative, pluralistic and accountable governance going ahead.

Speaking out in a Twitter space hosted by PTI's UK/US/Canada cars on December 3 2023, Barrister Khadija Siddiqi spotlights the neglected plight of female political workers arrested during the May 9 false flag. She questions why dozens continue to languish in jail without trial over six months later --unlike prompt bail grants for actual convicted criminals based on gender.

"What 'crime' did these women commit," she asks, "beyond refusing to buckle under pressure declaring Imran Khan incited violence that day?" She points out the impossibility of any such directives from the PTI chief when he remained under illegal detention throughout the protests. Yet rejecting the scripted accusations and excuses to release them has resulted in collective punishment, instead. "Mere support of PTI seems grounds enough for this endless penalisation without conviction," she highlights.

Siddiqi focuses attention on the tribulations of elderly prisoners like Rubina Jamil. The 60-year-old now depends upon her young son's assistance just to painfully climb into prison vans, shuttled from their bleak cells to superficial court appearances that never conclude their cases. By spotlighting Jamil's visible suffering, Siddique symbolises the psychological trauma inflicted without remorse upon all female political workers. "Where is due process, where is justice for these women, whose only stand seems a stubborn refusal to abandon their loyalties despite coercion?" she pointedly questions.

As 16 days of activism events commence, Siddique declines multiple speaker invitations in solidarity. "How can I attend functions abroad when people in Pakistan lack the courage to publicly advocate for wrongfully imprisoned women?" she asks.

Barrister Khadija Siddiqi highlights the contradiction of protesters arrested simply for peaceful assembly near cantonment areas suddenly facing charges of organised vandalism. "Those rounded up were not even instigators, yet now face endless jail time --unlike others freed if they publicly quit PTI and disparage Imran Khan."

Siddiqi appeals to the chief justice who honoured women's empowerment at his own oath-taking ceremony --"Yet where is due process or just treatment for prisoners specifically targeted as female supporters of an opposition movement?"

She dismisses the dragging legal proceedings as artificial constructions aiming to indefinitely detain dissenters without trial. Until given a fair court hearing to defend themselves, the truth stands captive to politically motivated narratives criminalising lawful assembly.

"Only free proceedings shall reveal the bogus nature of identical accusations and charges disproportionate to the reality of peaceful protests," she affirms. Until realisation of due process and rule of law, the defiant dream nurtured behind bars carries on, as darkness inevitably gives way to light.

Barrister Khadija Siddiqi calls upon all to keep raising voices for the plight of neglected female political prisoners. She urges the government to redirect focus from pursuing them as terrorists towards rebuilding the economy and rule of law.

"Endless witch-hunts only compound bitterness when due process gets abandoned and disproportionate force used against peaceful protestors," she warns.

Siddiqi highlights the emotional trauma heaped upon prisoners' families as well during restrictive visitations. "After hours of waiting, barely twenty minutes get granted --banning even simple handshakes or embraces with their loved ones wrongly incarcerated."

She appeals for more compassionate and humane treatment according to human rights principles, rather than vindictive collective punishment. Only by upholding justice and dignity for all citizens, without discrimination based on beliefs, can the state rebuild broken trust.

Siddiqi renews her plea for listeners worldwide to advocate along multiple platforms so the cries of female prisoners laying bare the systemic muzzling of dissent finally get heard. "Raise your voices with us until rule of law stands restored --when no one in Naya Pakistan needs fear arbitrary detention sans trial ever again."

Barrister Khadija Siddiqi asserts that irrespective of political affiliations, voices must unite for female prisoners denied basic rights. "The law says to bundle all relevant cases when arresting any accused. Yet our women face nominations in successive new cases as soon as bail gets granted in one."

Such procedural abuse, designed to prolong detentions, requires urgent judicial redress. "Our hope lies with the chief justice to restore rule of law --ensuring due process and proportionate application of justice regardless of beliefs or background."

She recalls the CJP underscoring female empowerment at his own swearing-in, insisting judicial oversight must end the misutilisation of state machinery to grind political axes and systematically dismantle opposition.

"The future of democracy itself in Pakistan now hinges upon checking political weaponisation of investigations and restoring sanctity of the constitution that promises equal rights to all citizens, regardless of party affiliation," Siddiqi affirms. She pins her hopes on the apex court to realign the scales of justice accordingly.

10

"WITHOUT LIBERTY I HAVE NOTHING LEFT TO USE EXCEPT MY BODY."

BELIEVING IN AND ADVOCATING FREEDOM

The quest for freedom permeates life itself. Whether animals pacing zoo cages or activists risking their lives at protest barricades, living beings share an innate desire for emancipation from imposed constraints that limit their ability to actualise free will. This irrepressible yearning catalyses struggles against structures of authoritarian control, injustice and oppression. As awareness of subjugation's injustice sparks, so too does resistance take shape, demanding recognition of fundamental liberties central to existence.

The natural world offers glimpses of this freedom imperative wired into lifeforms. Wild animals, when caged, grow remarkably restless, morose, and prone to physical deterioration, without the stimulation that exercising innate instincts in natural habitats provides. Marine creatures, like dolphins and orcas, display indicators of chronic psychological distress when captive, unable to traverse seas as their navigation systems promise. Birds confined in cages frequently get diagnosed with anxiety-induced conditions, due to their blocked ability to follow flight paths, etching their inner mapping across miles daily. Zoos now recognise that enabling species-specific freedom of movement, and enclosure similarities to native domains improves wellbeing, else captivity breeds illness beyond just physical safety. Through observable discontent, animals communicate a longing for emancipation from human-created confinement contravening their natural programming.

This biological push toward manifesting freedom permeates people, too, as self-awareness awakens the consciousness of subjugation's injustice over time. Across history, systems concentrating power in few hands, while marginalising vast majorities, inevitably cultivated dissent against normalised inequality. Every ideological evolution advancing rights began by disputing establishment tenets justifying stratified access, representation and participation as divinely pre-ordained. Yet the same innate conviction that dignity represents natural birthright kept sparking an uprising to reconstitute terms towards equitable balance. Most rebellions throughout history, regardless of outcome, channelled such yearning for throwing off internalised oppression's shackles. Even failed attempts left an indelible impact, expanding Overton windows to make way for future victories.

Spiritual traditions, over centuries, faced internal turmoil as adherents protested centralised authority over personal experience of the divine. Such demands for freedom of conscience and worship beyond institutional gatekeeping were perceived as explosive by religious orthodoxies whose arbiters guarded rituals and access to the sacred texts. But unrest, spearheaded by mystics and reformers, succeeded in revolutionising every major faith from within by restoring believers' direct interface with the holy, rather than fully depending on ceremonial interlocutors. Though punishments for the defiant ranged from excommunication to execution, the longing for unmediated divine communion mobilised the devout to transcend fears in order to reclaim personal spiritual agency. The echoes of their sacrifices continue empowering co-religionists today, bridling against arbitrary controls.

Visionaries through the ages recognised freedom's indispensability for collective advancement by emphasising voluntarism, self-determination, and systems leveraging consent over coercion to coordinate functioning societies. Governing philosophies enshrining individual autonomy and rights took shape to counter despotism's conflict-ridden instability. Watershed pacts, like the Magna Carta, upholding people's prerogatives above divine crowns, and later, independence manifestos by America's founders, reflected the realisation that pluralistic collaboration, foiled by inequality, inevitably fragmented. By framing freedom principles as bedrock for secure, prospering communities, they offered radical templates spurring worldwide claims for shedding colonial impositions next.

Freedom has thus invariably served as linchpin and rallying cry for epochal moments in emancipatory struggles, toppling oppressive structures once deemed invincible. From 18th-century revolutions ousting elitist monarchies, to anti-colonial movements dismantling violent occupations across 20th-century Africa and Asia, the idea of reclaiming human dignity and choice by dismantling coercive power catalysed surges towards civil liberties and sovereignty. Where brutal crackdowns followed, international solidarity evened the odds for agitators surviving, as inspirations like Gandhi and Mandela demonstrated. By recognising the collective capacity for self-rescue against designed disempowerment, their appeals turned freedom dreams into game-changing actualities, with oppositions and superpowers forced to relent before determined coalitions of the oppressed.

Today, freedom continues motivating frontline confrontation, with totalitarian forces unwilling to brook dissent in societies they dominate. China's cultural genocide against Turkic Muslims in Xinjiang detention camps faces rising global criticism alongside existing Tibet and Hong Kong solidarity. Strident civilian resistance also meets Myanmar's horrific ethnic cleansing of Rohingyas, or Taliban fundamentalism erasing hard-fought Afghan women's rights. Where repression by Syria's Bashar al-Assad, or Saudi bombing in Yemen tries violently quelling democratic aspirations, cries for self-determination swell further, internationalising these local struggles.

Palestinians remain steadfast, battling Israeli occupation amid West Bank apartheid governance and Gaza's open-air penal colony status, enforced through militarisation. Kashmiris defiantly demand ending India's brutal annexation, despite generations born and extinguished under the world's most intense clampdown. Their cause, lately won, renewed foreign policy interest as Modi's Hindu nationalism reveals totalitarian impulses. Across the spectrum, regimes banking on violence and surveillance alone to mute freedom dreams now face mounting grassroot, diplomatic and economic countermeasures, marking a global consciousness shift.

Pakistan's recent regime change crisis after Imran Khan's parliamentary ouster also spotlighted national outrage against perceived US-backed political interference. Khan's immense appeal across classes stemmed from espousing foreign policy independence from western pressures, plus anti-corruption drives seeking to empower grassroots. His framing the controversial dismissal as assault on sovereignty therefore activated mass protests, still enduring brutal police action. By defiantly upholding the right to self-determine leadership despite threats, opponents signal to global onlookers their refusal to accept covert circumvention of democratic mandate. Their readiness for street clashes to uphold electoral will echoes freedom struggles worldwide that refused bowing before forcibly installed orders.

Imran Khan frequently acknowledges his late mother's formative role in engendering his preoccupation with human freedom that shapes political goals to this day. He recalls her emphatic declarations about liberty constituting the highest pursuit for a meaningful existence on individual and collective levels. Internalising this as a child shaped Khan's ideological development, defending rights, questioning arbitrary controls, and opposing authoritarian constraints across personal, social and governance spheres.

As a high-profile sports celebrity who competed globally, Khan enjoyed rare autonomy and financial independence, granting options for self-definition unavailable to most. But privilege alone cannot explain his voluntary sacrificing of comforts for high-stakes political leadership and radical reform agenda, as mature democracies accommodate famous individuals without threatening power centres. That Khan chooses disruptive paths, including mass movements risking establishments' punitive retaliation, reflects a deeply embedded conviction about moral courage against injustice, which his mother highlighted as freedom's prerequisite.

The fearless defiance he displays against hostile campaigns by entrenched Interests threatened by his overhaul proposals --from national security prerogatives to elite privilege networks --gets commonly attributed by analysts to supreme self-belief or authoritarian tendencies. However, the root lies in absolute clarity about threats to sovereignty and people's will, constituting the gravest transgressions against the sacred compact between state and citizens in a democracy. His mother's teaching about protecting freedom above all instilled recognition that acquiescing before 'might is right' bullying, whether externally or internally imposed, represented the ultimate failure of leadership, dissolved public trust, and forfeited the right to govern or be governed fairly.

Hence, acquiescence or silence before oppression constitutes a cardinal sin, regardless of intimidation tactics employed by adversarial forces. This explains Khan's stubborn resistance as opposition leader against previous regimes, and during his own prime ministership, where he called out political machinations by the United States and allies designed to dictate terms skewed for western geostrategic interests, not bilateral respect. He frames all efforts at coercing Pakistan's leadership choices and policy directions through hybrid warfare tools like extra-constitutional regime change as direct assaults on the nation's hard-fought sovereignty after British colonial rule.

His mother nurtured a deep connection between personalised liberty and dignity with national independence and self-governance during childhood. This fuels his dramatic standoffs with superpowers through past anti-imperial alignments, including vigorous local protests against US drone strikes violating borders. He promised revisiting uneven partnerships, allowing external directions of Pakistan's international postures and security priorities beyond sovereign strategic welfare. And his commitment to safeguarding national sovereignty attracted diverse followers finding sincere resonance.

Now, his framing of the alleged western conspiracy, enabling his parliamentary overthrow, as a foreign-funded attack on freedom and democracy, has sparked strident civil disobedience. Khan's faithful, investing heavily in his vision for equitable development and corruption, accountability feel robbed of the right to self-determine leadership. His vocal stand for their mandate in turn earns their willingness to combat state violence to restore their electoral choice. This cycle strengthens Khan's storied position as a bulwark for ordinary citizens against powerful encroachers, both global and domestic --socialist leaders worldwide historically earned success on such positioning alone as defenders of sovereignty.

The courage to continually confront ruthless state machinery, including imprisonment and protestor deaths, while accusing western capitals, domestic political dynasties and military top brass of collusion, requires extraordinary conviction beyond everyday politics. Khan's unwillingness to compromise, despite knowing the tremendous odds stacked against him, relates to the central lesson his mother imparted -- that reclaiming freedom was paramount for securing rights and the non-negotiable duty of leadership. Through self-sacrifice, she emphasised ideals could triumph over material dominance.

Combined with faith anchoring his moral compass, this formative emphasis on liberty as foremost purpose, cultivated since childhood by his mother's wisdom, clarifies Khan's justification for high-stakes gambits, baffling analysts worldwide. Whether the unprecedented risk succeeds remains contingent on several factors beyond personal control. But the self-endangering defiance makes sense, knowing that for leaders like Khan, inheriting from predecessors who secured independence, capitulating before external or internal subversion of hard-won sovereignty is the ultimate failure of mission. His mother's voice thus launches battles defining Pakistan's future trajectory.

Without a doubt, Khan knows, whether facing down armored tanks in Tiananmen or innovating slogans honouring past generations slain mid-march, the existential drive for freedom rings eternally resilient. Its call for collective emancipation and co-authoring destiny ignores physical risks or historical odds repeatedly. Lost battles, as international solidarity shows, only redistribute courage before gathering storms. Freedom with responsibility thrives as a ceaseless human virtue, summoning moral power against each looming authoritarian darkness. Reclaiming dignity and choice makes life worth living beyond mere survival. Against its indomitable spirit, no regime thus lasts unchallenged as people ultimately seek autonomy's fulfilment over enslaving security beneath the boot. This truth reigns supreme, from the chained orca to the hunger-striking conscientious objector --defiance pumps lifeblood through creation's convoluted veins.

The defiant resolve to author this book, exposing inconvenient truths about Pakistan's deep state coercion resembles the mindset driving PTI's female political prisoners enduring illegal confinement. By refusing conditional freedom requiring public contrition, these captives claim moral victory through principled choice within restrictive contexts. Their empowering lesson --of fearlessly upholding truth irrespective of threats or suffering --mirrors the conviction propelling my literary labour to shed light on establishment excesses undermining civilian democracy. This shared commitment links my journey to those incarcerated women and the broader struggle for emancipation led by Imran Khan. It echoes the timeless seekers who embraced wisdom that real freedom dwells in freeing conscience from fear rather than just liberating physical bodies from cages. Like revolutionary figures throughout history, Khan and his grassroots vanguard internalised that mental autonomy thrives beyond bars and torture chambers, where souls still bent before tyranny remain shackled in meaningful ways.

My late father's defiance of regressive ancestral conventions also reflected adherence to personal liberty over conformity. He logically disputed norms not aligning with progressive world views, choosing to endure social sanctions. Walking his own path for him remained fundamental, even within restrictive environments, enabling fulfilment. His autonomous example, like Khan's decision to centre-stage controversial issues despite backlash, guided my choices writing this book. I cannot in good faith enjoy external liberties while self-censoring before threats intended to muzzle dissent. Khan's supporters battling state violence to protect their mandate also showcases that truly purposeful living springs from conquering fears.

I recognise that undertaking this work, elucidating the climate of intimidation, illegalities, and rights violations marring the democratic process risks nasty consequences for myself, too, in unjust systems rewarding sycophancy. Public awareness about coercion throttling free will angers establishments the world over. But hazily navigating through self-imposed filters to evade trouble forfeits the freedoms I wish to preserve by informing citizens. Like those female prisoners now central to Pakistan's political theatre, I accept that defending democratic values demands responsibility beyond personal costs. Their valiant incarceration despite options for early relief echoes the inspiration I draw from my father's model, resisting regressive diktats.

Ironically, Khan's chief oppressors as apparent architects of the regime change conspiracy epitomise the paradox between notional liberty and moral slavery to greed or power. The very top brass, undermining Pakistan's civilian mandate via extra-constitutional manoeuvres, appear captive to compulsions driving the worst authoritarian excess against citizens. Their willingness to enable civilian leadership changes forcibly every few years, revealing a lack of vision beyond seeking controls. Those falsely imprisoning opposition workers are pawns shackled by orders, never mind uniforms and the fear they inspire among detainees helpless before arbitrary system.

This underscores how oppressors forfeit freedom in profound ways, masked by illusory authority temporarily secured by might. In contrast, the very prisoners and banished leaders they persecute claim liberty through an unflinching adherence to truth and rights beyond material dominance.

Their autonomous choice earns inspiration and legitimacy outlasting current episodes. By weaponising compliance through handpicked collaborators, establishments expose their fundamental weakness rooted in denying citizens' sovereignty. But the latter's resilience returns to ignite change.

My father taught that authentic ownership derives from building rather than forcefully capturing. Khan's principled audacity challenges militarised political banditry now dominating Pakistan's chaotic trajectory. Through my book illuminating these coercive dealings eclipsing democratic freedom, I hope more citizens recognise that reclaiming rights requires not awaiting leadership but rather claiming identity as rights-holders themselves, first. This mindset shift, channelling fear into moral courage, can unlock shackles no regime imposes forever on people determined to stand freely as equals. Replacing Stockholm syndrome with participatory stewardship of community futures breaks cycles of authoritarianism relying on public resignation. Realigning national consciousness with transcendent yearnings for actualising freedom through non-violent, non-partisan sociopolitical activation, targeting systems, not individuals, constitutes lasting liberation.

Imran Khan's special leadership inspires artists like Omar Malik to dedicate their creative talents in supporting his cause:

When free-spirited artists like singer Omar Malik devote their emotive artistry and skills behind a political figure, it signifies the leader's exceptional magnetism. For it is not commonplace that creative souls given to carefree expression get drawn into partisan affairs unless profoundly stirred. That a youthful hometown musician is willing to risk his promising career, mainstream popularity, and even personal liberty to voice anthems lionising Imran Khan, reveals the latter's phenomenal persuasiveness. Clearly, Khan's upright integrity, selfless drive, and bold confrontation of entrenched tyrannical nexuses have ignited widespread public imagination. The sight of creative talents like Malik leveraging their stirring poetry, lyrics, and music to extol Khan's leadership signals his seismic impact as an authentic hope for the nation besieged by moral decay. Little surprise, then, that the young artist is intensely dedicated to Imran's cause with an almost reverent passion that transcends mortal electoral linkages between fans and politicians.

Omar Malik, a 32-year-old singer from Lahore, Pakistan, formally started his musical journey in 2012. He was the winner in the 2013 singing competition 'Voice of 103' in Pakistan and was a top contestant on 'Pakistan Idol' the same year. In 2014, Omar began his career as a music director and songwriter. He remains among the few lucky artists who got the invaluable chance to work with ace music composer Dr. Zeus from India. Moreover, he is the luckiest one to have his debut song released by India's leading music label, T-Series.

Malik's first song turned out to be a blockbuster, with over 15 million YouTube views. He has worked with the biggest record labels in Pakistan and internationally. Renowned names like Naseebo Lal from Pakistan, and legendary Bollywood star Akshay Kumar, have featured in Omar's songs. He sang 'Rabba' along with Akshay Kumar in the film 'Katputli'.

"I wrote and composed my first song for PTI and Imran Khan in 2013. Initially, my company had barred me from affiliating with any political party, so I would only write songs and direct music. But everything changed regime change conspiracy," shares Malik.

Malik wrote and composed nine songs for Imran Khan initially, including the viral hit 'Q Nikala Mujhy' that criticised Nawaz Sharif. However, after the regime change on 9 May 2023, Omar decided to openly sing for PTI as he felt it was his moral duty to stand for truth and justice. Malik says: "All of us, no matter our profession --as businessmen, writers, singers or workers --have a duty to stand by the truth. After 9th May, supporting Imran Khan openly became my ethical imperative."

Though many warned him not to associate with PTI, Malik asserts there can be no neutrality against injustice. His conscience compelled him to use his talent for the cause of truth.

The regime change completely transformed Malik's personal life, too. Once fun-loving, he now devotes himself fully to writing and singing for Imran Khan as he discovered a greater purpose. He fondly calls Imran Khan a 'spiritual father' who inspires his art. After 9 May, Omar has faced serious charges like terrorism for backing PTI. He and his family suffer due to false allegations.

"My conscience still doesn't allow me to stand by anyone but Khan sahab. 'Hum jaan denge, Khan nahi denge.' I have sacrificed my youth for Khan."

Malik vows to persist, just as his leader has never quit. He is optimistic about PTI's return and resuming his career ambitions someday. But he has no regrets prioritising the higher goals of truth and justice over his interests. Signing off with patriotic slogans, he quotes Imran Khan's line 'Mulk bhi mera, fauj bhi meri' to highlight his love for Pakistan.

The events of 9 May 2023 sent shockwaves through the political landscape of Pakistan. What started as a peaceful protest by PTI turned into chaos after clashes with police. Even months later, the full truth behind that tumultuous day remains uncertain, with conflicting narratives.

"I witnessed the horrific scenes at the protest rally on 9th May where police unleashed violence on peaceful PTI protesters including women and children. Like most PTI supporters, I was heartbroken seeing the inhumanity. It compelled me to raise my voice for justice.

"The authorities booked many PTI workers, including myself, under anti-terrorism charges which I believe were baseless and politically motivated allegations. We only exercised our democratic right to protest injustice, which should never be deemed terrorism in any civilised nation," asserts Malik.

In the aftermath, Malik decided to dedicate his music solely to speaking truth to power. His conscience propelled him to fight on, just like his leader, Imran Khan, who refused to give up despite arrests, protests bans and physical attacks.

"How could I remain neutral, seeing the fascism unfold against PTI and our leader? I joined PTI's struggle for haqeeqi azadi because we must stand up to oppression. On 9th May, injustice was perpetrated not just upon my party but upon democracy and ethics itself," Malik explains.

Through his lyrics now, Malik aims to capture the anguish as well as the hopes of PTI during its most turbulent chapter. He aspires to rally public spirit just as inspirational protest anthems did during the freedom struggle. No matter the risks, Malik intends to soldier on, singing for justice and Imran Khan.

For Omar Malik, backing Imran Khan's mission is not just political --it is personal. More than a party leader, Malik sees Khan as a guiding light steering the nation towards its destiny.

"Everything I am today is because of the man who taught me to dream big and have faith in my abilities --my spiritual father, Imran Khan," shares an emotional Malik.

Reminiscing about his early days, Malik reveals how, as a mere teenager back in 2013, he found himself disillusioned, wasting his creative talents partying without purpose. It was then that Imran Khan's rousing vision for Naya Pakistan ignited a spark in him. Inspired by Khan's patriotism and genuine desire to uplift the common man, music composer Malik felt stirred to wield his art for this cause bigger than himself. Soon he was writing nationalistic anthems supporting PTI, fusing modern sounds with traditional verse.

"I saw for the first time, a leader daring to speak truth to the powerful and shake corrupt cabals that bled our nation," says Malik. "While others mocked Khan, I recognised the greatness in the man willing to risk it all for higher ideals."

Over the years, Malik has seen his icon prove sceptics wrong again and again --via landmark projects, welfare schemes and global recognition, culminating in PTI's rise to government in 2018. He watched in awe as PM Khan enhanced Pakistan's prestige, despite internal efforts to destabilise his regime.

The ouster of his 'captain' left Malik dismayed but not defeated in spirit, thanks to Imran's resolve. No matter how great the odds against Khan, Malik's faith in his gumption remains unflinching. He vows to sing on, echoing IK's mantra: 'Don't give up till the last ball'!

Expanding on regime change, Malik is an ardent backer of Imran Khan; he attributes it to the leader's unflinching stand for Pakistan's rights and welfare. Unlike self-serving politicians, Khan's policies have always aligned with protecting national sovereignty, upholding the common man's prosperity and voice.

In Malik's view: "Imran Khan stands distinct as a statesman, shielding Pakistan's interests with courage --whether facing external pressures on independent foreign policy choices or internal mafias bleeding our economy."

Malik asserts: "When Khan speaks for Pakistan --its right to progress, sovereignty and self-respect --he voices sentiments of millions unable to articulate this dream haunted by exploitation narratives."

Unlike most leaders sweet-talking only during rallies, our leader, Khan, tenaciously pulled Pakistan onto the path of stability and global prestige through real structural reforms. Malik highlights game-changer steps like broadening tax nets, building world-class infrastructure, increased tech adoption for transparency and tapping Pakistan's tourism potential.

"Khan's vision for an independent, progressive Pakistan

aligned to its national interests attracts our generation," believes Omar Malik. He reiterates his unwavering stand behind Imran Khan for prioritising the needs of Pakistan's people and their right to determine its future. For Malik, Khan represents the peaceful democratic mobilisation of citizens long denied freedom from dynastic quasi-dictatorships in Pakistan's past.

Among his proudest moments was the day Omar Malik got the chance to perform his anthem live before the very leader who has been his muse for a decade now.

"Singing a song I composed specially for Khan on stage as he smiled and applauded holds an unmatched joy and sense of fulfilment for me," shares the young musician.

"I believe Imran Khan leads with empathy; he truly cares for the passions of those who stand by him through thick and thin. My leader's smile upon hearing my tribute makes every difficulty of this struggle worthwhile."

No matter how battered Pakistan's optimistic spirit may be in its current turmoil, Omar feels the light of hope will prevail --as long as brave hearts like his captain keep holding the torch high.

"Come what may, none can quell my voice raised for the righteous and for my beloved motherland. Pakistan Zindabad! Imran Khan Zindabad!" Malik proudly and loudly says.

11

"THERE IS SO MUCH DEBATE BOUT MODERATE AND RADICAL ISLAM BUT THERE IS ONLY ONE ISLAM"

UNDERSTANDING THE TRUTH OF ISLAM

I mran Khan in his book, Pakistan: A Personal History, writes:
"When I was older, I found Iqbal's work hugely inspirational. He argued against an unquestioning acceptance of western democracy as the self-governing model and instead suggested that by following the rules of Islam, a society would tend naturally towards social justice, tolerance, peace and equality. Iqbal's interpretation of Islam differs very widely from the narrow meaning that is sometimes given to it. For Iqbal, Islam is not just the name for certain beliefs and forms of worship. The difference between a Muslim and a non-Muslim is not merely a theological one --it is a difference of a fundamental attitude towards life."

Islam emerged in Arabia in the 7th century CE as a monotheistic Abrahamic faith centred around belief in the one God (Allah) and Muhammad (PBUH) as God's final prophet. Its core teachings emphasised justice, equality, compassion for humanity, and moral uprightness. Islamic theology upholds Allah as omnipotent, omniscient, and the force animating all existence. Key principles include strict monotheism, acts of worship and devotion such as daily prayer and fasting, emphasis on intention and deeds in this life to attain heaven in the afterlife, charity, and looking after less fortunate members of the community.

Islam's central text is the Quran, comprising revelations received by Prophet Muhammad (PBUH). Other key sources on law and guidance are the Hadith, or documented traditions and sayings of the Prophet and his Companions that inform everything from jurisprudence to daily living. Muslims also revere notable prophets recognised in Christianity and Judaism, like Abraham, Moses and Jesus Christ, as important messengers of the same God, even if their messages became corrupted over time. This continuity anchors Islam as an Abrahamic faith.

Within a century after the Prophet's death, Islam spread rapidly, building one of history's largest empires spanning the Near East, Central Asia, North Africa and parts of Europe. This allowed interaction and syncretism between classical Islamic thought and Hellenistic, Persian and Indian civilisations over centuries. Islamic civilisation made seminal contributions in fields as diverse as mathematics, optics, medicine, architecture and philosophy that shaped Medieval Europe.

Today, Islam dominates North Africa, the Near East, Central Asia, and parts of South and Southeast Asia. Sizeable Muslim populations reside across Asia, Europe and the Americas due to both historical and ongoing migration. As Islam's populations grow globally, Muslims confront rising Islamophobia in many non-Muslim majority nations, especially the west.

Since the 9/11 attacks specifically, Islamophobia features mainstream political rhetoric and media narratives in many western nations. Both geopolitical interventions in Iraq and Afghanistan, plus domestic terror attacks like the 2015 Paris shootings, shape Islamophobic discourses that frame Muslims as threats. This drives repression, ranging from cultural stigmatisation to racial violence targeting local Muslim populations.

Western societies have seen bans on traditional religious clothing like burqas and turbans under the pretense of secularism and integration, but perceived by Muslims as cultural erasure. Surveillance policies focused on mosques, Muslim communities, and travellers perceived to "look Muslim" have become normalised security policy in America and Europe, despite their racist undertones.

Hate crimes, from threatening letters to physical assaults against Muslims, spike after major terror incidents. Young Muslims face bullying in schools while adults deal with employment and housing discrimination, driven by Islamophobic biases. Polls consistently show Muslims named as the most feared, least liked, and most suspicious religious community across much of the western world.

This toxic environment has profound psychosocial impacts on western Muslim populations -especially visible minority immigrants and their children -who contend with identity struggles, alienation and dependence on tightly knit ethno-religious support systems as coping mechanisms against pervasive exclusion and hostility from society at large.

Some argue this marginalisation of Muslim diaspora communities in the west fosters insularity and extremism among youths struggling with identity and belonging. In that context, Islamist radicalisation emerges from a search for purpose and fraternity. While only tiny fractions pursue violence, the Islamophobic social backdrop undoubtedly fuels receptivity towards extremism.

Countering Islamophobia has thus become central for leaders seeking peaceful integration and resilience among western Muslim communities, against radicalisation risks. Among the most vocal opponents of Islamophobia on the world stage has been Imran Khan, the former prime minister of the world's second largest Muslim country, Pakistan. Khan has repeatedly called out the double standards applied towards Muslims and Muslim-majority countries by western nations while stressing the need to address root injustices enabling extremism.

His most forceful critique came in his speech at the 74th United Nations General Assembly in September 2019. Khan asserted that Islamophobia had grown exponentially across the western world in the nearly two decades since 9/11. He argued that this stemmed from the selective framing of violence and terrorism as Islamic problems uniquely, which bred negative perceptions and hostility against Muslims en masse.

Khan called this out as patently unjust, given no other community is collectively blamed for the actions of disturbed individuals sharing aspects of identity or self-professed ideology not endorsed by mainstream thought leaders. He gave the analogy of mass shooters in America rarely being portrayed as representing all whites, Christians, or right-wingers even if claiming inspiration from those identities.

The Oxford-educated former sports celebrity called on western governments to match their rhetoric of tolerance and liberalism by proactively protecting the rights, freedoms and dignities of Muslim citizens facing increased bigotry. Insensitivity towards religious symbols like hijabs, or racial profiling policies targeting Muslims, should have no place in enlightened secular democracies.

Khan asserted that far-right hate groups propagating fear and violence against Muslims were being normalised in political discourses rather than marginalised like they ought to be in democratic societies. He pointed to unequal applications of security policies focused on Muslims, which amounted to institutionalised prejudice, violating assumptions of racial or religious equality.

The Pakistani leader also called for acknowledging the shared responsibility of former colonial powers and recent military interventions for exacerbating conflict fault-lines across the Muslim world. Over four million Muslims have died due to wars in Iraq, Syria, Libya and Afghanistan over the past three decades. Khan attributed this horrific violence to a combination of western policy blunders aligned with regional dictatorships, which shattered these societies while fuelling cycles of radicalisation and terrorism.

He called out the active western enablement of extremism through past policies, like backing Mujahedeen groups against the Soviets. Later instances of indirect military aid to extremist factions fighting regimes opposed to western interests, despite knowing consequences, illustrated ongoing complicity. By turning a blind eye or actively enabling radicals when geopolitically convenient, western governments effectively became cocktail partners for breeding extremism globally. The violent blowback was inevitable.

Khan concluded by calling for sincere inter-civilisational dialogue and reforms to foster harmony. Within Muslim societies, that meant living up to spiritual tenets of compassion and justice. Externally, ending interventions to sow chaos and instead addressing historical injustices. For western powers, it required honesty about past policy failures, rethinking antagonistic policies while standing up against Islamophobia and xenophobia.

The former cricket star's speech drew praise globally as a powerful call-out against the systematic mainstreaming of Islamophobia by powerful interests across the western world, both in narratives and policies. He effectively broadened culpability for radicalisation beyond violent extremists themselves, to equally implicate policy failures and pervasive societal discrimination against Muslims by western liberal democracies not practicing their own stated values.

His speech's significance endures despite losing power in Pakistan, partly due to tensions with western governments over his assertive rhetoric. Currently imprisoned over disputed charges of misuse of public donations for political rallies that critics allege as trumped up, Khan's bold legacy of speaking against the oppression of Muslims remains widely admired, especially across the Muslim world. His warnings of the dangerous symbiosis between community discrimination and radicalisation still resonates, for leaders seeking to overcome both global terrorism and rising intolerance.

Throughout Islamic nations' histories, Muslim leaders with strong religious and moral grounding have inspired intense loyalty and activism among supporters. When these principles come under pressure from secular or external forces seeking to undermine legitimacy, the popular resolve to protect leaders and Islamic conservative ideals becomes a powerful factor. From Erbakan in the 1990s to Erdoğan against modern-day coup attempts -and clear parallels visible in Imran Khan's own standoffs today -these patterns span decades.

Necmettin Erbakan's Welfare Party represented Turkey's Islamic resurgence in the mid-1990s, much as Khan's PTI has tapped into religio-conservative undercurrents long suppressed in Pakistani politics. Both awakened visions of sovereignty and national strength tied to Islamic identity. However, radical secularism in Turkey's military and elite establishment conspired against this movement through what some termed "postmodern military coups". Media and big business interests aligned against Erbakan's agenda -reminiscent of Pakistan's establishment striking against Khan's vision over fears of power, ebbing away from entrenched bureaucratic circles and liberal elites.

Erdoğan came to be seen as redemption for the embattled Islamic cause when he split from Erbakan's party to form the AKP, while asserting Turkey's Muslim heritage as compatible with democracy. Khan, too, bases his vision on an Islamic system situated within electoral principles -seeking to balance religion with global realities. Erdoğan framed his role as reversing sanitisation of faith under past state policy -not dissimilar to Khan's standing firm against western cultural impositions that clash with Pakistan's identity. Both leaders' vocal defiance of secularist elite notions around religion struck deep chords across conservative masses and working classes while rattling bureaucratic coterie.

AKP is the Justice and Development Party in Turkey (Adalet ve Kalkınma Partisi). It's the party founded by Recep Tayyip Erdoğan, and currently headed by him as well. Media commentary framed sentiments rejecting AKP as defence of lifestyles against creeping "Talibanisation"- reminiscent of Khan misrepresentations.

Khan's removal echoes patterns where leaders uplifting religious values coordinated elite pushback, powered by secular lobbies and external powers feeling their interests jeopardised. Supporter outrage stems from witnessing in-groups repeatedly subvert leaders they elected, based on shared principles and policies reflecting spiritual worldviews removed from day-to-day governance for so long.

Popular outcry against the Turkish military's 2016 power-grab set Erdoğan apart as an embodiment of the public will -a Sufi-inspired vision centred in Islamic historical identity and sovereignty now under existential threat. Millions took to the streets and gathered outside airport runways, beating pots and pans amidst gunfire -answering Erdoğan's FaceTime call and proudly reclaiming ownership of political space against tyrannical encroachment. Khan's protestors express similar passions -vocal minorities unwilling to stay silent when representative leaderships articulating religious standpoints get controversially ejected without convincing technical grounds.

Both leaders' defiant strength amidst sustained pressure

campaigns resonates with supporters' conceptions of resolute Muslim leadership, facing down authoritarian state capture. Their vocal stands are reminders for disenfranchised publics to reclaim agency, when elite machinations appear geared towards muting citizens' preferences for faithful policymakers. Supporters feel connected by the shared experience of resisting establishment gaslighting, dismissing religious sentiments as irrational or destabilising, remaining steadfast even when gaslit as brainwashed masses becomes its own badge of honour and act of resistance.

Calls for Islam have deep roots in populations' genuine mainstream beliefs, long trivialised and suppressed from policy priority. Supporters interpret bombastic declarations by bespoke westernized circles lambasting religious rhetoric as further demonstration of the cultural disconnect that necessitates vocal leadership, giving political centre-stage to voters' authentic priorities, grounded in shared Muslim heritage and decolonised identity.

Both leaders have more controversially invoked the language of holy war and martyrdom amidst security crackdowns -evoking symbolic, religious imagery that critics take at face value as incitement, despite its primary aim being to rile up sentiment and signal unwavering commitment to facing down threats. Supporters broadly understand such coded messaging framed around rally-the-base defensive posturing, rather than literal calls to violence. They resonate with the spirit of kindred forces desperately working to beat back domineering institutional power, demanding submission and obedience from elected leaders actually representing voters. Leaders uplifting religious grassroots see their mandates challenged by establishments wielding legal-bureaucratic tools to undermine power shifts, countervailing their institutional interests. Khan and Erdoğan form archetypes of such leaders leaning into issues, symbols, and rhetoric, carrying significant weight among large conservative groundswells long distant from governance access. This galvanises passionate movements interpreting such signals as their values and identity, finally gaining political centre-stage against elite institutional indifference to their preferences and priorities for far too long in their democracies.

Where secular establishments wield nexuses of influence across state institutions and old-money circles as an ecosystem punishing policy agendas, giving voice and space to religious populations, intense resentment builds. Defiant defence of leaders directly symbolising the promise of representational access becomes an outlet for these groups to vent frustrations over being perennially politically sidelined and culturally delegitimised for simply carrying non-cosmopolitan or non-elite identities and beliefs.

So, in present-day clashes around Khan and Erdoğan, their incensed, faithful supporters come largely from places of shared trauma and group pain, over secular state highhandedness against religious political forces. Their intense loyalty and extraordinary sacrifice stems from the resolve these towering figures have come to symbolise: the dream of politically and culturally de-stigmatised Muslim identities and citizenries no longer excluded, spoken down to or institutionally policed for electorally seeking leaders boldly prioritising agendas reflecting supporters' faith-rooted needs and perspectives.

Like my leader, Imran Khan, my father embodied the true Islamic values of humanity and humility in his character and conduct. For him, Islam had always been a religion of compassion -evident through acts of kindness towards rich and poor alike. Though not a wealthy man himself, he made it a point to give generously to those in need -be it impoverished tenants, village beggars, or orphaned street children getting coins every Friday. He drew no lines between Muslims and non-Muslims when distributing his limited means, for in his belief, charity uplifted humanity.

At times, there would be scarcely any money left for our family after he was done supporting others. Yet that selfless service brought him joy and fulfilment. In my father's eyes, this was the only way to present the beautiful spirit of our faith and alter misperceptions -through wordless deeds reflecting universal love and care for the vulnerable, irrespective of creed or background. His lived example shaped my understanding of Islam as a religion devoted to lifting the weak and spreading mercy.

I firmly believe that if all Muslims began sincerely exemplifying the religion's core values of humanity and compassion in their conduct -as embodied by leading lights like my father, Imran Khan, and certain enlightened Islamic leaders -the faith's glorious ethos would speak for itself. There would no longer be room left for anyone to sully Islam's image or misconstrue its teachings.

When devotion translates into acts of selfless service and boundless care for the suffering or destitute -be they Muslim or otherwise -it powerfully brings the Quran's sublime values to life. Every genuinely charitable deed rooted in the empathy and grace that Prophet Muhammad (PBUH) modelled chips away hardened perceptions. In place of fear or hostility towards the Islamic faith, hearts organically fill with admiration for its palpable wisdom and beauty.

Islam has been a beacon of equality, dignity and compassionate justice throughout history when rightly practised. If present-day Muslims were to lead their lives exemplifying the same lofty morals they preached, and ensured welfare for all in early Muslim societies, no amount of agenda-driven propaganda could distort reality. Both Muslims and non-Muslims would viscerally experience the humanistic Islam, following in the footsteps of all Prophets of God. From that personal taste and Islam's tangible fruits, all misgivings fade.

As I conclude this chapter, I want to emphasise how, even from prison, Imran Khan's resolute conviction continues to rattle the political elite. Detention has not dampened his fighting spirit against corruption and misgovernance. The poem that follows symbolises how his enemies cower before Khan's resilience, faith, and principled stand -an unbreakable determination fuelled by the very fact that truth speaks loudest from places of greatest suppression. Through this poem, I aim to capture the fire of his courage that intensifies when justice is denied.

Behind Bars, A Lion Heart

Caged yet defiant, his enemies cower,
Resolute in spirit, his courage towers.
Patience of prophets, the courage of Ali,
Ardent disciple of truth and harmony.
Beloved by masses, devote hearts enshrine,
Guided from heavens with will divine.
No tyrants prevail against the righteous wave,
Peaceful but potent, the noble and brave.
In victory or trial may his mettle stay strong,
Upholding justice his lifelong song.
For my leader, Imran Khan.

12

"ARE WE PAKISTANIS, CHILDREN OF A LESSER GOD"

REJECTING OPPRESSION AND DOUBLE STANDARDS

O ften painfully, humanity comes to gradually realise that systemic oppression and double standards deeply entrenched in our societies yield immense suffering. As awareness grows around long-overlooked issues, more people awaken to these injustices that devalue and dehumanise groups seen as "other".

Recent instances have sparked global backlash over marginalisation baked into narratives and discourse -whether western media is framing conflicts in more sympathetic terms for those of certain privileged ethnicities or nationalities. Outrage ensued when a journalist portrayed Ukraine war refugees as more shockingly relatable due to their "blue eyes and blonde hair" unlike crisis-stricken Middle Easterners or Africans eliciting little outrage over the years.

Public pushback has also intensified against false propaganda that demonises oppressed groups or strips context from their plight. For example, rights organisations condemned BBC's coverage of Israeli airstrikes on Palestinian children as obfuscating facts on the ground and breeding misinformation.

After strong criticism, retractions followed. But immense work remains to remedy such normalisation of oppression across world conflicts.

These instances highlight that when racist, orientalist biases govern reporting or crisis responses, otherwise ethical societies can remain silent for appallingly long. But a light now shines on this darkness as people realise that no human being anywhere deserves different standards for life, dignity and compassion based on ethnicity, faith or nationality. All of humanity must make this perilous collective journey towards addressing the injustices we ignore or even perpetuate through our institutions, media ecosystems and policies. The liberation of the oppressed and building unity across manmade divides remains imperative work for citizens worldwide in this era.

It heartens me deeply to see bold, principled leaders across domains risk their careers and platforms to challenge entrenched injustice narratives. Figures like journalist Mehdi Hasan daringly expose hard truths through probing questions that confront disinformation or state propaganda aimed at manufacturing consent for the oppression of marginalised groups worldwide. His journalistic ethos embodies speaking truth to power.

So too do several celebrities and public figures stand up for ethical causes opposing the mighty, out of sheer conviction - despite pressures to remain silent on controversial issues. For example, football icon Cristiano Ronaldo stridently amplifies messages supporting relief for Gazan children suffering apartheid. Supermodel Gigi Hadid similarly leverages her catwalk fame and global fandom to regularly advocate for Palestinian rights and dignity.

Other stars criticising Israeli occupation include actresses Gal Gadot and Melissa Barrera from their influential positions within Hollywood and Latinx entertainment. Such stars leverage their brand clout and visibility to drive hard conversations challenging normalised injustices, even at the risk of their careers. British comedians, television personalities and acclaimed actors like Steve Coogan are also vocal, calling to boycott apartheid through ethical activism that pressures their institutions and establishments towards progress, despite threats or censorship.

These pioneering voices serve as moral compasses, guiding global society towards a more just future by refusing complicity with oppressive status quos - even at great personal risk. Their integrity to resist cruel injustice, despite daunting opposition, offers both protective cover and inspirational blueprint for others capable of leverage to follow suit in solidarity.

Particularly, those in institutions tacitly furthering systemic inequity from privileged perches of authority, have additional responsibility for reforms. Be it politicians legislating, corporations setting workplace policies, academics shaping young minds, or religious leaders providing pastoral care - silence and inaction equals complicity.

Lone voices of conscience standing defiantly apart first endure ridicule, then violent backlash as authoritarian structures, feeling threatened, close ranks. Still they pierce the veil of fear and conformity slowly, emboldening the cautious, giving vocabulary to the voiceless. By weathering the wilderness years, undermining cultural prejudice through truth's appeal to innate decency in all peoples, these glowing flames of moral courage gradually swell towards vibrant wildfire.

Their sacrifice transforms team sports, segregated schools, apartheid republics and patriarchal professions by awakening the slumbering conscience of majorities too distracted by busy survival to confront normalised oppression earlier. Once awakened, the hunger for fairness and empathy swells every human heart. First brave activists, then growing numbers within every community do shine light, piercing darkness, guided by stars who show audacity of spirit, transcending mortal limits.

It is also encouraging when heads of state, despite external pressures, leverage their global platforms to advocate rights and dignity for oppressed groups. For instance, Turkish President Erdoğan consistently champions the Palestinian cause at the United Nations, risking relationships with powerful entities to oppose the egregious occupation. Malaysia outspokenly leads initiatives defending Palestinian children and statehood rights as a moral duty of Muslim governments.

Ireland has also embraced legislation banning goods from illegal settlements -one of Europe's strongest responses affirming action, despite Israel's ties with western states. Meanwhile, South Africa strongly mirrors the Palestinian plight as akin to its own Apartheid struggle under Madiba, and remains vocal in keeping hopes alive for self-determination. Even the African Union and its members rally for Palestinian statehood and necessary reforms each year. Such rare, principled leadership on the highest levels serves as an ethical model for the entire international system. It compels the world's conscience to ask difficult questions on its failings thus far that enable the persistence of atrocities against civilian populations without recourse. Their advocacy calls us to look within first, before seeking change outside -be it around civilian protection laws or possible deterrence steps for occupier states violating countless conventions.

These states also set valuable precedents toward appropriate responsibility sharing, rather than abandoning the vulnerable. Their solidarity reflects the spirit of Bandung unity, espoused by post-colonial Asian and African leaders decades ago. And it incarnates the Islamic principles of uplifting the marginalised, regardless of parochial political interests.

My leader, Imran Khan, has never backed down from

speaking truth to power against oppression, no matter the opponents or consequences. His impassioned advocacy for civilian casualties, victims of US drone strikes in Pakistan's Waziristan region, reverberated globally. Khan was among the first prominent voices confronting superpowers by unambiguously calling out the devastation and deaths of innocent Pakistanis from covert bombing raids as an unacceptable breach of sovereignty and humanitarian norms.

His bold and crisp statement rejecting complicity - "Absolutely Not!" -won hearts for its moral clarity and force of conviction. These words became a rallying cry, woven into national memory and identity. Pakistanis emblazoned the defiant phrase across t-shirts, car bumpers, banners and shop fronts -icons of resistance against imperialism and rallying behind indigenous leaders upholding dignity.

Khan gave human faces, stories, and dignity to economically disadvantaged villagers in northwest Pakistan, whose lives and identities got devalued as "collateral damage". His advocacy called out the horrific double standards where loss of brown, Muslim lives elicits little outrage compared to similar military actions elsewhere. It highlighted the intersection of poverty, race and geopolitics enabling such routine violence by powerful states upon the world's weakest with impunity. Indeed, Khan emerged as perhaps the first prominent national leader in Pakistan's history to courageously advocate for the basic rights and dignity of marginalised groups that past ruling parties had encouraged oppression against, or negligently overlooked at best.

Whether it was rendering tribal Pashtuns in FATA as second-class citizens deprived of lawful protections for decades under the guise of "strategic depth," or the brutal military crackdown on demands for rights by Baloch people, ruling establishments maintained an iron grip that Khan boldly confronted, despite threats.

Similarly, where past governments readily offered Pakistan's land and air space for western wars in Afghanistan, like a client state with little regard for consequences, Khan refused such complicity that repeatedly brought mass civilian misery next door. He instead championed pursuing peaceful resolutions to stabilise Afghanistan, aware of blowbacks at home.

In essence, his stances upheld the welfare and lives of ordinary Pakistani citizens above narrow geopolitical profiteering or security state dictates. This revealed a devotion to uplifting the marginalised and improving real citizens' wellbeing unmatched by previous figurehead leaders who largely served elite western interests while public conditions stagnated.

Much like Jinnah remarkably stood tall for persecuted minorities when political opportunism dictated otherwise, Khan today risks his platform and very political capital to speak unpalatably bold truths against all manifestations of totalitarian establishments operating with impunity within Pakistan's borders -whether in restive zones or worrying oversteps stifling dissent.

Such advocacy upholding even dissidents' basic rights and demanding accountability reveals a leader walking the talk on the constitutional protections for which Pakistan's visionary founder had laid the foundations. It rekindles hopes amongst citizens that the egalitarian welfare state Jinnah had envisioned may yet transform into reality, given sincere leadership, personifying his ideals with clarity and courage again.

Unlike privileged politicians alternating between government bungalows and overseas havens, Khan resonates as a leader living and breathing alongside everyday citizens. He reiterates his resolve to stand firmly rooted in native soil no matter the fallout:-"Who leaves their homeland?" As such, Khan attracts grassroots talent like Murad Saeed, Ali

Muhammad Khan and Shehryar Afridi into PTI's ranks rather than just recycling dynastic elites.

However, when the going got tough, with establishments conspiring regime change, opportunists blitzkrieg-defected as Fawad Chaudhry did. This vindicated Khan's war philosophy - it's only in adversity that one knows real allies over fair-weather friends. Yet, Khan isn't bitter towards former confidantes abandoning ship under pressures. With trademark composure, he gracefully accepts some mistakes, judging characters wrongly. But the litmus tests of loyalty have granted him clarity on who to marshal for the long haul.

This episode, and initial high-hope stalwarts, have taught Khan vital lessons on investing authority in indigenous leaders deeply rooted in their soil and communities. Such organically arising representation brings integrity versus parachuting, in electable but duplicitous cadres. It also furthers PTI's vision for delivering governance reflecting grassroots realities and uplifting communities long neglected by disconnected ruling classes.

Where past governments brazenly looted state coffers through dynastic corruption as ordinary Pakistanis struggled, Khan worked earnestly to uplift downtrodden citizens during his administration. From spearheading Langar Khanas, offering humanitarian shelter and dignity to the homeless, to rolling out health insurance cards, allowing impoverished families access to quality medical care -he prioritised relieving widespread public suffering that callous regimes had normalised.

Unlike aloof ministers barricaded in lavish villas, Khan personally visited shelters housing destitute citizens, to listen and share meals with them on the floor as equals. These gestures humanised governance, signalling the highest office cared for the everyday Ramzans, Fatimas, and Rehmans who constitute Pakistan's soul. It reflected leadership by example - ministers expected to serve people hands-on.

This posited a vision of good governance accountable to grassroots versus just elite-driven agendas. Is it then any wonder oppressed communities see hope in a leader touching their wounds directly, instead of ruling through feudal intermediaries and privilege? One who leads with empathy and uplifts the weakest to transform across-the-board public welfare?

When has Pakistan's power ecosystem ever permitted such dangerous humanity and solidarity with the disenfranchised before brutal backlash ensued? But the exploited and struggling recognise in Khan -flaws notwithstanding -a tenderness reminiscent of Prophet Muhammad's (SAWW) blessed leadership. And they intuit his words arise from walking alongside them till the nation's old wounds of inequity heal.

In his years as opposition leader, then premier, Khan fought for electoral reforms such as electronic voting to eliminate rigging, decades of subverting Pakistan's democracy. The establishment saw his grassroots enthusiasm as threats to the controlled rotation of patronage governments operating for their benefit. Hence their severe opposition to e-voting and a leader awakening public scrutiny over institutional controls. But Khan remained steadfast, crusading against the puppet-show electoral theatre cyclically disenfranchising citizens from genuine choice or voice in governance made 'for the people'.

Now, through an unprecedented mobilisation in the face of his ouster as an elected PM, Khan's journey from head of government to political prisoner fuelled by a repressive regime has only amplified mass questioning. Millions now openly challenge the coercive state apparatus that has covertly orchestrated Pakistan's 'political' landscape since inception while concealing citizens' reality behind hollow slogans, broken promises and divisive propaganda.

Finally, Pakistan's public has grasped the stage-managed theatrical masks, generational establishment oppression sabotaging their will while usurping their right to craft national destiny through genuine representatives. Imran Khan's resistance first as premier, now from behind bars, tore off that persistent facade -opening people's eyes to their denial of self-determination and voice by unaccountable centres of hard power through the very ruling setup claiming to defend constitutional democracy and civilian supremacy. His struggle laid bare contradictions between Pakistan's law, rights, and founding vision, versus systemic unlawful dominance over all.

Among Khan's important electoral demands was enabling millions of overseas Pakistanis to feasibly vote from abroad, given their national stakeholds. However, self-serving regimes thriving on mass disenfranchisement unsurprisingly denied this reasonable expansion of electoral access.

The immediacy of late journalist Arshad Sharif's words, ominously warning of shadowy forces behind such decisions, still shakes hearts. He sacrificed his life uplifting taboo truths to liberate public consciousness from coercion cloaked as choice. Arshad's defiant ideology and smiling face may be cruelly silenced, but his legacy only grows as forbidden questions surge. Millions now sense how intricately managed elite interests dominate governance, arbitrarily denying their basic rights like diaspora voting.

So when earlier regimes touted inflated claims of democratisation while repeatedly smothering free and fair electoral conduct, Khan emerged as an antithesis, upending establishment rulebooks. His incisive rallying cries since imprisonment indict undemocratic monopolies usurping citizens' dreams under the guise of democracy. The awakened urgency his movement stoked for Pakistan's true freedom, rights and self-realisation cannot be extinguished -only to blaze forward Arshad's hopes for an equitably just homeland. The journey is arduous, but determined flames are igniting historical inequities into ashes.

My father lived his values with quiet conviction in a world full of injustice. He had no tolerance for double standards or hypocrisy that valued appearance and status over integrity and compassion. Even as my mother would plead for him to buy new suits befitting his station, he would demur -how could he indulge in frivolous shows of wealth when the poor struggled to survive right on our own doorstep? He chose, instead, to dress simply and donate excess means to those in need.

Attending social events clad in his trademark grey or burgundy waistcoat thrown over a crisp white shalwar kameez, his style was understated yet elegant. More importantly, it was a statement of his principles -substance matters over superficiality, humility over false appearances. He judged people not by their material prosperity but by their character. Arrogance, greed, insensitivity disgusted him; such self-absorbed posturing was the essence of what he considered evil, in this world rife with double standards favouring the rich and powerful. If he disliked someone, he would refrain from interacting with them rather than put on a façade of friendliness -nothing could make him complicit in the prevailing culture of insincerity. His blunt honesty could seem caustic, but it upheld what he cared about most: -integrity and human dignity. In a cynical world where many resign themselves to hypocrisy for status or survival, my father had the courage to reject false compromises. His was a life anchored in speaking and living the truth as he saw it. I dare not sully his memory by justifying those he openly condemned when alive. Doubly so when his criticisms targeted not people themselves but the double standards enabling prejudice and oppression. Right until the end, he worked to uplift the vulnerable. To honour his legacy, I must carry forward that effort in my own way, however long that struggle may be.

While my father and iconic leaders like Gandhi made profound personal sacrifices to remain true to their noble principles, Imran Khan's journey exposes similar conviction and courage at yet another level.

As a highly successful cricketing hero who brought Pakistan global glory on the pitch, Khan enjoyed enormous popularity and a comfortable life. Yet in his athletic prime, he turned to building a cancer hospital to help save impoverished patients unable to afford urgent treatment. To raise staggering funds for the mammoth philanthropic Shaukat Khanum project, he exhausted himself campaigning globally. Where other megastars might have retired in smug contentment, basking in fame and riches, Khan devoted his profile and energies to serving the poor, despite enduring mockery from critics doubting his seriousness.

Later, when he entered the cutthroat arena of politics seeking to reform the corrupt system throttling his country, Khan once more invited immense hostility and propaganda. With his wholesome reputation for integrity, he posed a direct threat to powerful entrenched interests enriching themselves for decades by bleeding dry the nation's critical resources. They subjected him to character assassination, even physical violence that once put his life at risk. He persevered undeterred -galvanising the disaffected youth with his vision for a "Naya Pakistan," predicated on social justice and the rule of law.

While all odds seemed stacked against his idealistic movement, Khan drew strength from the moral force of being on the right side of history. His honesty and mass appeal ultimately triumphed at the polls, for him to become prime minister against an opposition accustomed to capturing power through deceit, bribes and nepotism. However, effecting genuine reform requires dismantling deeply corrupt structures

-thus once more pitting Khan against nefarious elements determined to see his government fail at any cost. He continues that long march, guided solely by "Iman, taqwa, insaaf," -the same faith, self-discipline and principles of justice my late father stood unflinchingly for all his humble life.

13

"THE WAR ON TERROR IS THE MOST INSANE AND IMMORAL WAR OF ALL TIME"
REJECTING VIOLENCE AND EXTREMISM

The struggles of Palestinians and tribal Pashtuns spotlight how years of unaddressed injustice can mutate legitimate grievances into extremism, especially among youth deprived of hope. When loved ones and homelands are ravaged with impunity, some will inevitably advocate for revenge, regardless of civilian cost. While their violent methods targeting innocents deserve condemnation as counterproductive and morally bankrupt -so too do the initial oppressions and denial of rights that breed such hatred.

Hamas undoubtedly commits reprehensible acts of terror by indiscriminate rocket attacks on Israeli population centres. But preceding its ascent were decades of Palestinians losing homes, lands and lives under Israel's occupation and aggressive settlement expansions in blatant violation of international law. These historical realities get erased in media narratives painting Hamas as irrational aggressors, rather than as a tragic embodiment of despair morphing into extremism.

Similarly, Pakistan's problematic military operations and US drone strikes have killed countless Pashtun civilians unjustly labeled as militants -from newly born infants to helpless elderly citizens -creating profound grievances. When teens grow up orphaned by bombardments that decimate entire families without accountability, we must acknowledge the seeds of violent hatred sown even as we categorically oppose terrorist methods targeting civilians in revenge.

Reductive tropes of intrinsically violent Muslims or Pashtuns ignore how generations ravaged by unbridled state aggression can spawn radicalised factions, however morally bankrupt. Before decrying the revenge philosophies of Hamas or the Taliban, the world must also show concern for enabling root causes:-occupation and subjugation. Global media coverage remains selective, vilifying armed reactionaries struggling against oppression but rarely forcing spotlight on their oppressors who initiate catastrophic conditions. We collectively fail our shared humanity if conditioned to readily denounce the violence of the weak but stay silent regarding violence derived from power. Breaking this hypocritical media paradigm demands moral courage to write truthfully, asking more complex questions about causes fuelling tragic effects.

Here is a profound point:-few of us pause to consider how casually normalised stereotypes and insensitive humor targeting disadvantaged groups quietly perform a dehumanising function, building negative perceptions over time to justify discrimination. Fortunately, in every generation, history produces some courageous voices, rooted in their own experience of oppression, who confront such profiling at great personal sacrifice. Their activism gradually refutes toxic misrepresentations by introducing voices of conscience that bend the moral arc towards justice.

African Americans endured brutal slavery in a country idealising liberty, only to suffer another century of being denied basic rights after abolition. Against this traumatic backdrop, creative black talent, from jazz pioneers to athletes, shouldered hopes of proving their community's worth.

Performers like Nina Simone lent soul-stirring defiance to the civil rights anthems, while scholars like W.E.B Dubois intellectually dismantled myths of inherent racial inferiority. Maya Angelou articulated how poverty and trauma bred desperation rather than any cultural depravity. Muhammad Ali shouted his rage at white hypocrisy from the boxing ring, sacrificing his prime years to prison when refusing military service in a racist army. Nina Simone broke from a dazzling career to perform protest songs, facing violent retaliation, while writers Alice Walker and Toni Morrison amplified stories of resilience by black women triumphing over unthinkable exploitation. Their collective work countered news reports demonising protests against oppression as nothing more than anarchic riots justifying police brutality.

In India, where rampant colourism fuels prejudice against darker-skinned citizens as backward or impure, visionaries like Dr. B.R. Ambedkar and Periyar fought for legal protections. They ignited grassroots movements to reclaim the dignity of those marginalised by arbitrary divisions of birth -from 'untouchability' to inter-caste violence against those daring love marriages. Simultaneously, poets and musicians spread messages affirming beauty in diversity -that pigmentation carried no correlation with human potential. Regional cinema gradually offered more empowering portrayals to fuel societal introspection.

While blondes became subject to crass objectification in popular culture, pioneers like Monroe owned their sexuality as agency in a patriarchy, rather than victimhood. Athletes, like tennis legend Billie Jean King similarly smashed stereotypes of female frailty in sports. Sikh jokes, attacking turbans or beards obscures how symbols foster communal identity for a diaspora facing post 9/11 persecution, until educators like Lily Singh and Jay Shetty emerged on mainstream platforms to replace reductive assumptions with nuanced cultural insights. Behind every cruel caricature lies untold stories of trauma and resilience. If we can discover our shared humanity in each journey, empathy dissolves reductive typecasting into forgiveness, which alone can heal the world.

Some thought-provoking questions that challenge prevailing assumptions: why do nations wielding unprecedented global power, and claiming commitment to peace, so often pursue policies promoting violent conflict instead? A pattern emerges where profiteering interests of weapon manufacturers hold greater sway in political corridors than ethical considerations for human dignity or diplomacy. Visionaries daring to advocate alternative solutions centred on de-escalation and uplifting the oppressed get falsely maligned as sympathisers of extremism. We witnessed this through the Iraq war, Afghanistan, and now amidst the Palestinian crisis - where simply upholding humanitarian law elicits unreasonable backlash.

Imran Khan currently endures vile propaganda, equating his criticism of heavy-handed state policies that enable extremism to somehow endorsing terrorism. This requires blatantly ignoring how his government facilitated fence-mending dialogue with groups harbouring legitimate grievances against past military actions. Prioritising reconciliation over retribution is the only sustainable way to counter militancy, even if parties on all sides dissatisfied with the status quo resist compromises. But Khan's bold gamble for peace threatened arms manufacturers and hawkish establishments seeking to perpetuate cycles of conflict in the region to enrich personal interests. Powerful western actors share culpability in this self-serving machinery, churning out endless wars under various guises. The Afghanistan invasion and the destruction of Iraq on concocted weapons of mass destruction (WMD) lies resulted in millions of innocents killed, displacement, and regional chaos fuelling new terrorist outfits.

Yet no reparations, let alone apologies, have occurred for the lies and loss. Instead, leaders - who speak frankly against this deadly military industrial complex, retaining authority through violence and division - get punished. We witnessed similar ousting of icons like Mossadegh of Iran, or Patrice Lumumba of the Democratic Republic of the Congo (then known as the Republic of the Congo), who pursued independent economic policies empowering their people over foreign exploiters. The prevalence of this suppressive model explains why movements for peace routinely face subversion.

The above two are historical examples of democratically elected leaders from developing countries who were illegally removed from power in coups backed by western governments seeking control over those nations' natural resources and assets.

Mohammad Mossadegh was Iran's prime minister in the early 1950s. He advocated nationalising Iran's oil industry to ensure profits went towards uplifting the Iranian people, rather than simply enriching British corporations who had controlled and reaped the benefits from Iran's oil prior to that.

His push for economic sovereignty threatened western oil interests, who lobbied intelligence agencies in the US and the UK to orchestrate his forcible removal in a 1953 coup, installing a dictatorial Shah instead. This fuelled resentment towards external meddling, eventually resulting in the 1979 Islamic revolution against the Shah's authoritarianism.

Similarly, Patrice Lumumba became an anti-colonial icon as the Congo's first democratically elected prime minister in 1960, after pushing for genuine independence from brutal Belgian rule. Like Mossadegh, he sought autonomous economic policies focusing wealth gains towards alleviating poverty and developing the Congo for its own citizens' welfare, rather than allowing ex-imperial powers to continue exploiting resources and income streams.

Within months, Lumumba was deposed, and was assassinated in 1961 through Belgian-backed political unrest and mutiny. Historical records confirm the CIA were among the external parties involved in ousting him to undermine the emergence of an independent, self-determining African country serving its own people over Cold War resource control priorities. His murder destroyed hopes for true Congo independence.

Both underscore when emerging leaders in geostrategic nations work against neocolonial economic systems favouring former imperialist countries. Covert plans eliminate them from power and install more compliant regimes -setting back self-determination and welfare reforms for decades in the aftermath of political instability. It explains the distrust of western 'pro-democracy' rhetoric, given the horrific precedents.

For things to change, we must reform not individual figureheads, but entire systems, thriving by holding humanity hostage to fear psychosis while profiting from sales of weapons. Supporting leaders with conscience, critical of unethical status quos, provide hope for resisting the march towards catastrophe. For peace can only prevail through upholding justice and human rights universally.

My father and my leader offered sage advice to read between the lines when assessing the pronouncements of the powerful. The need to vocally reaffirm virtues reveals lurking doubts over the erosion of public trust -why explicitly deny politics influences military leadership unless growing accusations necessitate damage control? Periodic reassurances of loving the Pakistani people and enjoying their support suggests creeping anxiety over waning credibility from past overreaches. Simply trusting these press statements as sincere would be naïve when actions have repeatedly contradicted democratic principles or accountability.

We witnessed similar dynamics when the Bush

administration insisted intelligence had conclusively confirmed Iraq held weapons of mass destruction. The more they protested, thinking otherwise to be foolish, the hollower their words rang when the invasion's ghastly aftermath revealed zero evidence of any WMD program. Yet by then, they faced no consequences for a war started on lies, causing incalculable suffering. Across history, tyranny soils its hands then desperately clutches at ethical facades cracking under the strain.

Whether military rule in Pakistan, or superpowers invading weaker states, the playbook remains the same:-brute force and oppression thinly veiled by propaganda about benevolent intentions. And the public often wilfully accepts these claims, finding comfort in trusting establishment narratives rather than asking tough questions to speak truth to power. After all, accepting that systems entrusted with incredible responsibility can operate with callous disregard for human rights or dignity proves deeply unsettling. We would rather explain away uncomfortable facts than confront the magnitude of institutional failures.

But as my father and leader understood, silence and selective blindness only enables the continuation of exploitation. If leaders must dedicate precious time insisting of their virtue, investigating the repeated rights violations that elicited this crisis of credibility is the citizenry's solemn duty. Though difficult - and even dangerous, when exposing the methods underpinning power, transparency remains the sole disinfectant for abuse. Else, our failure to question the narratives and intentions of the powerful reduces democracy to mere illusion.

Imran Khan deserves immense credit for boldly denouncing the so-called US-led "War on Terror" as deeply unethical and counterproductive right from its inception after the 9/11 attacks. Long before public opinion caught up, he expressed grave concerns about military strategies prioritising brute vengeance over addressing root causes that radicalise factions into extremism. His firm anti-war stance stemmed from a rare combination of humanitarian sensibilities, strategic acumen, and courage of conviction. Khan compellingly argued that bombing inhabited regions into oblivion, while causing civilian carnage inevitably breeds more desperate militants. Without providing viable political endgames to remedy factors instigating militancy, tactical gains ring hollow. Furthermore, he rejected the implicit bigotry in stereotyping any violent group claiming Islamist ideology as representing mainstream Muslims worldwide. Painting diverse cultures with the broad stroke of assumed guilt by association is unjust, and provides terrorist propaganda material, targeting disaffected diaspora youth attracted to radicalisation.

Instead, Khan has long advocated for military disengagement and reconciliation, prioritising negotiated settlements wherever viable. Groups arising from unaddressed political disputes require credible promises of representation and rights reform. Where conflicts stem from occupation, either territorial negotiations or power-sharing arrangements must occur under independent arbitration. Dictating terms of surrender to weaker groups through overwhelming firepower generally backfires. Peace endures only by elevating the exploited, not forcing submission.

From Iraq to Palestine and the tribal Pashtun regions in his native Pakistan, Khan bravely opposes military action that harms civilians already oppressed by conflict. His principled positions frequently draw vitriol both from pro-war western interests and also hardliners in his homeland. But facts vindicate his stance:-Iraq's destruction birthed ISIS while the Taliban resuscitated, following two decades of gruelling occupation. A true leader places people over profits, cooperation above ego-driven domination. The world desperately requires such moral courage at policy levels before our shared future gets sacrificed in flames of hatred and arms industry profits.

Let's highlight a sobering truth:-those advocating for peace often face the harshest crackdowns because their message of conflict resolution threatens powerful interests thriving on perpetuating violence. Imran Khan currently endures state persecution through false accusations, arrests and alleged torture for seeking negotiated settlements with groups harbouring legitimate grievances. His aim of alleviating the exploitation that radicalises the aggrieved threatens the extremists wanting ongoing war, and also the establishment factions profiting from property grabs in ravaged areas.

We witnessed similar neutralisation of peacemakers throughout history. Gandhi was repeatedly imprisoned by the British Raj, while his movement, employing non-violent civil disobedience, sought India's liberation. Imperial exploiters denounced him as traitorous for demanding basic rights and dignity for his people. Later, Martin Luther King Jr. met federal persecution, violence, and ultimately assassination for promoting integration over the status quo of racial segregation preserving white privilege. Those reaping unchecked power or profits from oppressing vulnerable populations always oppose voices enlightening victims towards seeking equitable redress.

While sanctimoniously flaunting facades lauding peace, they simultaneously undermine organic leaders capable of uniting everyday people to non-violently challenge totalitarian structures. Because acknowledging legitimate dissent risks unveiling ugly truths of minority rule through unethical means. Whether colonial plantations built on slavery, or arms sales to conflict zones, or illegal territorial occupation, profiteers cannot tolerate transparency exposing sordid secrets. If facts revealed the ongoing oppression fuelling radicalisation, global opinion could demand policy reforms jeopardising elite capitalism.

Thus, the powerful resort to maligning calls for conflict resolution as appeasement of extremists. By distorting the messenger, they hope to kill his unifying message of redemption through upholding justice as the path for sustainable peace. But such desperate censorship only validates the urgency of dissent they try suppressing. For humanity to survive its own capacity for tyranny, we must have the collective courage to defend those daring to speak truth to power rather than stand silently by during their persecution.

Now, let us highlight a salient point:-how leaders who consistently question the establishment after retirement immediately flee abroad, while Imran Khan alone chooses to stay rooted, facing persecution. This reveals much about the state's transparency and tolerance of dissent. We have seen a pattern of army chiefs settling overseas post-retirement, despite decades of power and perks extracted locally. Musharraf lived comfortably abroad, shielded from accountability for emergency rule arrests and rights violations avoided through exile. Retired generals leverage state privilege to enable offspring dual citizenship and assets stashed globally.

What patriotism do such figures exhibit in amassing wealth through public office then conveniently abandoning ship the moment accountability pressures surface? Do their family members not utilise local infrastructure and subsidies prior to migrating? Clearly the expectation is to keep enjoying internationally mobile lifestyles. Khan remains an exception - anchoring himself despite risks of imprisonment and alleged torture.

And why is Nawaz unable to furnish legitimate evidence justifying his fortune built by plundering state industries amidst stints in power? Neither daughters asked to account for offshore holdings? Zardari never explaining Swiss cases? All pontificate about democracy's fate, yet refuse transparency themselves.

Established plunderers who mouth platitudes defending the state in fact systematically exploit it like personal fiefdom, knowing consequences are evadable. Then they project doubters, who endure persecution without absconding, as lacking patriotism! Before denigrating Imran Khan's loyalty, all other power brokers must first explain their own accountability. Why promising the poor roti, kapra, makaan, if only prioritising securing the wealth, health and lifestyles of their own brood instead? Such are the farcical theatrics played out by alleged upholders of national interest to disguise self-interest.

14

"FAITH WITHOUT WISDOM AND KNOWLEDGE COULD PRODUCE BIGOTS COMPLETELY LACKING IN COMPASSION AND TOLERANCE"

DEVELOPING WISDOM

Faith is defined as complete trust or confidence in something or someone. It signifies belief in or devoted allegiance towards a certain principle, cause or spiritual conviction. Faith is belief without tangible evidence or material confirmation. It stems from a profound inner knowing:-the existence of truths beyond rational demonstration or scientific proof.

The concept of faith often relates to religious or spiritual worldviews, accepting beliefs based on teachings or sacred texts considered divinely inspired rather than rationally derived. Adherents demonstrate faith by fully entrusting in these beliefs as a guiding compass, aligning thoughts and actions accordingly. Pilgrimages, rituals, relics or worship rituals all symbolise expressions of devout faith within diverse religious traditions globally. Faith signifies loyalty to a living community of believers bound by a shared higher purpose and destiny transcending mortal lives.

However, faith need not apply solely in theological contexts. Any individual, group or movement powered by intense commitment to a vision based on core principles or philosophies opposed to status quos demonstrates conviction stemming from resolute faith. Champions of civil rights, political revolutionaries, social reformers or conscientious objectors all exhibit deep-rooted faith in their respective causes. Willingness to endure ostracization, persecution or even martyrdom arises from staunch faith in the ultimate righteousness and triumph of their worldview that spurs determined action.

Sceptics consider faith irrational and even delusional, given the lack of irrefutable evidence. But for the faithful, inner knowing suffices as the bedrock of perceived reality more vital than rational theories. Where facts threaten belief systems, faith enables compartmentalisation to sustain loyalty to doctrines. Faith can therein turn dogmatic if defensive rather than based on confident truth. Blind allegiance ignores conscience, making devotees susceptible to manipulation towards extreme polarisation or violence by charismatic demagogues appealing to threatened belief constructs and base emotional instincts.

But alternatively, sincere faith, centred on universal love and elevated human consciousness, can achieve unprecedented unity, inspiration and social transformation. Faith based on inclusiveness, compassion and service can uplift humanity, provided that intolerance of alternate perspectives gets avoided. Viewed thus, faith signifies aligning to higher wisdom by transcending ego. Ultimate reality remains forever unknowable -so faith simply offers varied paths to relate to that unsolved mystery.

Wisdom distinguishes itself from mere knowledge by signifying discernment, applying broad understanding towards exercising prudent judgement. Knowledge deals with gathering facts, information and empirical evidence about the world. Wisdom leverages knowledge for optimal analysis towards taking actions aligned with positive virtues to produce constructive outcomes.

Thus, being knowledgeable contrasts with being wise. Knowledge accumulation alone risks being superficial, amoral or even enabling harm if devoid of humanistic insight or empathy. Wisdom balances cold logic with the warmth of intuitive emotions. It overrides selfish ego to uphold the public good. A wise person envisions the moral dimensions and consequences of choices beyond limited personal advantage.

The paradox of having expertise without wisdom frequently manifests in careers like law, business, politics and even academia. Highly trained professionals sometimes utilise skills towards unethical practices due to detached displays of technical prowess devoid of ethical grounding. Wisdom would entail employing expertise to advance social justice causes instead. Skills ought to support solving problems afflicting humanity, not exacerbate inequity and suffering. Seeking wisdom requires lifelong commitment, patience and introspection. Since perfect objectivity remains impossible for finite minds, continuous self-critique checks subjective limitations. This mitigates the pride preceding a fall. Some features of a wise person include balanced emotional maturity, nuanced perspectives accounting for context, and masses' welfare centralising decisions. Quieting destructive emotions and desires allows intuition to guide behaviour free from egoistic impulses or materialism.

By advancing morally conscious policymaking, elders and advisors counselling through sage advice can establish wisdom-centred governance models. Such treasuring of experiential insight protects against reckless application of knowledge and youthful impulse. From jurisprudence to statecraft, such scaffolds preserve unity and progress. Ultimately, wisdom seeks to uphold ethical responsibilities between communities, societies, and humanity's collective legacy across generations.

Most fundamentally, knowledge deals with assembling verified facts and theories towards describing reality and the natural world accurately. The scientific method established specialised processes for acquiring systematic knowledge based on impartial gathering and testing of evidence. Accepting or debating claims now required replicable, measurable data. This birthed the era of modern science prioritising logic and reason.

Before definitive science, traditional knowledge systems and folk wisdom offered early epistemology grounded in customs, rituals and anecdotal experiences making sense of life's mysteries. Elders interpreted events and phenomena through mythological frameworks hallowed by ancestry and oral histories. Cohesive worldviews took shape from collectively held assumptions and common sense observations, in accordance with intuitive reasoning.

While often imprecise, such symbolic knowledge still offered early civilisations functional guidance regarding values, livelihoods and social order. Customary laws based on practice, tributary relationships and mythic moral precedents enabled community stability, despite the lack of deductive investigation. Intimate ecological wisdom also accumulated from directly inhabiting lands over generations. But absent impartial analysis, subjective bias went unchecked. Superstitious beliefs proliferated around issues like health, despite the lack of cause-effect understanding. Societies splintered over resistance to updating flawed traditional knowledge or accommodating dissent. Modern scientific inquiry thus revolutionised discovery by emphasising evidence. Facts now required proof through rigorous experimentation, not just appeals to questionable authority. Blind adherence to dogma slowly gave way to continually updated, peer-reviewed investigation across expanding disciplines.

Yet the ascendance of information also birthed detachment from holistic meaning. Specialisation fractures interrelated worlds into silos, losing contextual wisdom. Quantifying the empirical universe still leaves existential yearnings unreconciled. Beyond materialism, questions of purpose and ethics linger. The more humanity decoded external world complexity, the less life coherence remained internally. Information alone cannot mandate morality or meaning. Therein lies the limits of knowledge untempered by compassion or conscience. Integrating scientific capacity with humanistic wisdom promises our best hope for constructive future evolution, while distinct concepts, faith, wisdom and knowledge remain deeply intertwined for humanity's decision matrix navigating the ontological journey. No one faculty alone suffices for optimum equilibrium between ideological security, situationally appropriate action and intelligible frames comprehending complex realities. Imbalance risks extremism, instability and chaos.

Faith grounds against nihilism by positing connective tissue to enduring purpose and community. But unchecked zealotry makes faith woolly rather than illuminating. Wisdom contextualises situations morally, upholding ethical responsibilities. Yet subjective biases blur wise analysis if not tested. Knowledge erects interpretative pillars through evidence but blinds without insight. Still, factless faith offers false consolation.

Each concept checks the excesses of the other for necessary integration. Faith needs wisdom, directing love's surrender towards responsibility and service. Knowledge enables wisdom to inspect biases and upgrade. Where knowledge and wisdom grow estranged from faith, the inner world destabilises. For sustainable flourishing, human capacities need unified application. No single capacity alone unlocks our ultimate potential.

The unifying strand remains recognising inherent human dignity and common destiny. Whether invoked as divine brotherhood in faith traditions, or commonwealth securing legal rights, or scientific facts confirming biological family -all progress uplifts collective sentience. No matter which faculty takes theoretical precedence, aiding human welfare through ethical means fulfils their constructive purpose. Our joint fate hinges upon each capacity harmonising to transmute ephemeral mortality into enduring legacy. The application determines their combined fruitfulness.

Imran Khan's unique life journey manifests a rare embodiment of faith, idealism, service, courage and sacrifice converging into wisdom-driven policies uplifting humanity, his international acclaim as a legendary sports champion never diverting him from passionate mega-scale philanthropy projects. Fundraising global citizen initiatives against climate catastrophe already reflected sage priorities transcending ego gratification. By risking name, fame, comfort, and simple contentment towards championing revolutionary reforms as a political leader, Khan personifies a profound commitment to his vision for collective dignity and justice, regardless of the hostility this invokes from deeply vested interests. Such focused moral clarity arises from a bedrock of genuine spiritual faith or else succumbs to backlash.

In Khan's own words, authentic faith mandates alignment to higher truth and virtue. His consistent opposition to unjust wars in the face of propaganda, profiteering and even death threats demonstrates conviction beyond personal costs or benefits. By upholding the equal status and rights of all citizens, rather than exploiting identity fault lines for political capital, he transcends tribal ego towards wisdom, placing shared humanity first. Khan's faith fuels his tireless exertion to empower the marginalised: not through empty promises or populist handouts, but through sustainable system reforms securing equal opportunities, transparency and social security, irrespective of privilege. Faith devoid of responsible conduct means nothing to him. Actions validate belief.

Simultaneously, Khan combines faith-based idealism with judicious compromise through wisdom accumulated from governance experience, expert counsel and self-critique. Blind absolutism gives way to nuanced policymaking, navigating unavoidable limitations and constrained resources in imperfect scenarios. Reckless revolutionary zeal, endangering stability, gets tempered by cautious incrementalism, building constituencies and fortifying institutions vital for sustained nation building. The vision remains unwavering but strategies adapt contextually between short-term survival needs and enduring structural change.

Khan likewise demonstrates the consistent will to update flawed traditional assumptions by embracing modern tools and scientific problem-solving -from pandemic management to environmental analysis to data transparency initiatives. Information aids moral governance. Rejecting superstitions or unfounded stereotypes reveals commitment to verifiable reality and proof-based policymaking -the foundation for knowledge-centred leadership. But technical expertise alone cannot address moral questions of ethics and positive civilisational values which shape human welfare. Therein arises the balance where wisdom harnesses knowledge to advance conscientious statecraft for the public good.

Contrast this against bigotry arising from unchecked dogma rooted in ego gratification rather than authentic spirituality. The demagogue panders to negative identity constructs, demonising imagined threats from vulnerable outgroups. The populist clings to superstitions impeding social progress and doubles down by suppressing dissenting knowledge. Such politicking may draw mass hysteria, but invariably causes division and deterioration rather than positive transformation.

Conversely, Khan's vision for Pakistan's national revival, and his current resistance movement, seek to mobilise diverse citizens, especially youth, towards reclaiming their sovereign democratic rights and rebuilding national institutions on ethical foundations, serving all citizens equally. This uplifting posture eschews the exploitation of fault lines between gender, ethnicity, creed or class, which only serve to divide ordinary people against collective interests. Only the politics of hope, unity, responsibility and redemption can birth a just order securing welfare and dignity for our progeny. Through his principled stances and transformative vision transcending division, Khan manifests leadership combining faith with wisdom and knowledge in balanced measure to manifest compassion.

As the daughter raised by a discerning father of strong moral compass and intellectual depth, I inherited a legacy of critical examination towards events and leaders professing visions for societal reform. Father taught me that extracting surface meaning from lofty pronouncements remains insufficient to gauge authentic leadership. One must assess integrity of conduct beyond rhetoric; over time, across contexts. Do actions flow from mere hungry ambition and clever opportunism or some profound commitment to principles that compels particular paths involving sacrifice? I apply these yardsticks studying Pakistan's convoluted political history and conclude that Imran Khan stands apart, based on his track record.

My book undertakes an analytical inquiry into Khan's extraordinary life trajectory, for readers to conduct their own reasoned evaluation regarding his sincerity. Unlike most leaders' rise to power through privilege, ruthless cunning, or cultivating backers for quid pro quo, Khan risked his world acclaim as a sports superstar, his comfortable lifestyle and even his domestic popularity to relentlessly advocate reforms targeting systemic exploitation and misgovernance by status quo elites. Where self-interest would dictate acquiescence to enrich self and family through corruption conducted with impunity by predecessors, Khan raged against the decay such degeneracy, bred in state institutions and public morality. He willingly accepted pariah status during a decade-long struggle as critics mocked his political prospects.

Father's wisdom guided my exploration of context, causality and longer arcs beyond the headlines to uncover truth. I traced Khan's fierce hostility towards hypocrisy and double standards in governance as a consistent thread back to his college days, where he confronted racism in England. His refusal to ingratiate powerful local bullies reflected his adherence to integrity regardless of popularity, foreshadowing his defiant independence against corrupt mafias dominating national leadership. His commitment to lifting marginalised communities persisted through world cup victories, building Pakistan's premier philanthropic cancer hospital, and his global advocacy against crippling debts hampering developing nations' self-reliance hopes.

This recurring cycle of leveraging privileges, opportunities or crisis moments to uplift vulnerable groups reveals a profound humanitarian faith animating Khan's worldview. His compassion resists exploitation by consistently voicing concerns of the oppressed. Thus, entering politics became the inevitable next phase in this crusade to structurally transform broken governance failing most citizens through institutional reforms centred on transparency and justice. The goal has always remained empowering the disenfranchised majority to take ownership in national destiny, his positions favouring peace, dialogue and non-violence a steady commitment to principle over politically profitable warmongering. This track record earns him alone the credibility to be torch-bearer against expanding tyranny. Readers can weigh the evidence chronicled in this neutral examination to draw their own conclusions on sincerity. But Khan's life evidences a wisdom transcending vanity and knowledge directed by conscience:-hallmarks of an enlightened leadership faithful to democratic justice.

NOTE OF HOPE

I finish this book with a renewed sense of optimism that my leader, Imran Khan, and all political prisoners, will be released and exonerated sooner rather than later. As time passes, the political landscape in Pakistan is experiencing rapid shifts indicating a momentum change in Khan's favour.

This positive momentum was sparked by the Supreme Court's recent dismissal of the high-profile "cipher" case against Khan and former foreign minister, Shah Mahmood Qureshi. The controversial case relates to diplomatic cables between Islamabad and Washington, which Khan claims exposed a US-led conspiracy to overthrow his elected government through a parliamentary coup in April 2022.

By waving around an alleged cipher during public rallies, Khan was accused of unlawfully disclosing official secrets and abetting acts against the state. However, the exaggerated charges have now been thrown out by Supreme Court Justice Athar Minallah, who defiantly told local newspapers: "Imran Khan has not been found guilty; he is innocent."

Justice Minallah said there was "no proof" that Khan's actions benefited any foreign country. This has been interpreted as a significant rebuke of the current caretaker setup and the past coalition government, which legal experts suggest only pursued the cipher case for political gain to intimidate the wildly popular opposition leader.

With the dismissal of the state secrets case, pressure is mounting for authorities to release Khan's close aides and other political prisoners caught up in what he calls "politically motivated" cases against his Pakistan Tehreek-e-Insaf (PTI) party.

However, the arrest and harassment of PTI workers have spiked noticeably before election. Videos widely shared on social media show police tearing up nomination papers and physically preventing female PTI candidates from submitting election forms.

This crackdown comes ahead of a new general election ordered to take place on 8 February 2024. The PTI has already launched its campaign through online Jalsas for this landmark contest, which most objective observers believe will result in another landslide victory for Imran Khan's populist, anti-corruption platform.

The PTI's appeal stems largely from Khan's personality and uncompromising efforts to end dynastic politics, fight economic inequality, and enhance Pakistan's sovereignty. Unlike the tainted, family-run parties that previously dominated national politics for 30 years, Khan is seen as a relatively clean, reform-oriented leader committed to justice and the rule of law.

This divergence helps explain why PTI parliamentarians and activists increasingly face arbitrary arrests, beatings, and legal harassment at the hands of a nervous state apparatus. It also demonstrates why the Supreme Court's decision to exonerate Khan in the cipher case is such a game-changer. Already, his bail ruling has reinvigorated PTI supporters, who sense the establishment is losing its grip.

Assuming February 2024's election takes place in a reasonably free and fair environment, Khan appears primed to embark on a second term as prime minister, this time with a stronger democratic mandate for implementing his promised reforms targeting tax evasion, judicial corruption, and the stagnant economy handicapped by nepotism. He may also revive foreign policy priorities aimed at enhancing Pakistan's geopolitical neutrality.

None of this will be achievable without first securing the release of political prisoners and tempering state institutions seemingly acting at the current government's behest to harass opposition voices. The recent exemption of Khan from charges in the cipher case was a step in the right direction. But authorities must also drop dozens of questionable legal cases against PTI parliamentarians, local councillors and grassroots organisers.

Provided partisan meddling in the justice system and security agencies can be curtailed, Pakistan appears back on track to give Khan another opportunity to lead the country following February 2024's make-or-break election. Despite ongoing political turbulence, the Supreme Court's pushback against his legal persecution points to brighter days ahead.

As justice slowly prevails, there is room for hope that Khan and all other opposition voices will soon be freed from this political witch hunt. That could open the door for a groundswell of popular support to coalesce behind his PTI party's platform of anti-corruption, social justice, economic relief, and secure borders guided by a balanced foreign policy.

With Khan no longer constrained by the cipher case, or other spurious charges designed explicitly to thwart his ascendancy, exciting new possibilities lie ahead for Pakistani democracy after enduring months of instability. The light at the end of the tunnel could be Khan's reinstatement as prime minister on the back of an electoral mandate cementing his position as the subcontinent's most trusted political actor. Khan possesses one formidable advantage: he remains by far Pakistan's most popular politician, while his opponents are largely discredited as an unlikeable rogues gallery of kleptocratic families dominated by the criminally convicted. So if Khan and his PTI can overcome systemic obstacles and an institutional deck stacked against them, his redemption story will truly capture the imagination of justice-seeking citizens at home and abroad.

With the deck increasingly stacked against the ruling regime, the Supreme Court verdict granting bail to Khan has opened up space for cautious hope that the remainder of this elongated electoral cycle can unfold freely and fairly. Pakistan desperately needs trusted leadership and progressive reforms to fix its broken economy, lift some 100 million citizens out of grinding poverty, and regain prestige on the world stage.

An impartial 2024 election culminating in Khan's return could rekindle Pakistan's economic and social aspirations after so much recent turbulence. More immediately, a court decision paved the way for his embattled party members to regroup and launch their postponed campaigns without harassment. But tough obstacles persist due to the establishment old guard's unwillingness to forfeit its historical dominance over national politics.

As citizens shaken by a year of upheaval pin their hopes on Khan's exoneration as a springboard to launch his political revival, all institutions must respect the primacy of electoral transparency and the voice of the people. Allowing an unshackled campaign on a genuinely level playing pitch, followed by voting without backroom manipulation, is Pakistan's only path out of this long crisis of governance that predates even Imran Khan's entry into politics.

With the Supreme Court setting a principled tone, and popular opinion firmly on the side of change, elements wedded to preserving their privileges at any cost face shrinking options to once again undermine the popular mandate.

As this pivotal election cycle moves into high gear, the judiciary and all organs of the state must now follow the Supreme Court's lead by ending harassment of opposition politicians, their supporters and campaign staff. Shutting down legal avenues to further destabilise politics would signal a much-needed closure to an unsavoury chapter of persecuting certain voices who dared to challenge deep vested interests jealously guarding the status quo since Pakistan's birth.

My hope upon finishing this book is for total political liberation and that justice be granted, not only to opposition stalwarts who stood their ground, like Imran Khan, but to all prisoners of conscience across society. Pakistan's chronic governance problems stem fundamentally from the lack of accountability and the deficiency of genuine representation at leadership levels. Khan's exoneration will mark a good start, but freeing politics from pernicious external constraints is the only way for electoral democracy to bloom.

As the countdown now begins for the next government-defining general election, there is no room left for further extra-political interruptions to upend the mandate of Pakistanis hungering for prosperity, security, and international prestige following years of misrule by indicted private interests masquerading as public representatives.

My prayer upon ending this book is for Pakistan's future trajectory to be put back in the hands of voters where it belongs, rather than manipulated through orders delivered by unelected actors in smoke-filled rooms. Justice must not only be done but seen to be done by decisively stopping all forms of interference with politics and governance beyond what the constitution expressly allows.

Upholding genuine democracy to reflect the will of the masses and bringing detractors as well as manipulators fully into its ambit is Pakistan's only remedy to break out of the current cycle of instability exacerbated by constant extra-political interruptions for vested interests. With fresh elections guaranteed and meddling firmly red-lined, some national healing can begin.

I will finish this book on the optimistic note that better days lie ahead for the judiciary to build on welcome steps. Strengthening electoral integrity and safeguarding each citizen's vote to freely shape the country's path forms a critical foundation. Rule of law, not of power brokers, must prevail for Pakistan to progress.

I end this book quoting the inspiring words of my leader, Imran Khan, who once said: -"Either you surrender or you fight till the end". He has clearly chosen the latter.

Khan continues to valiantly fight against injustice, corruption and lawlessness. The nation is proud of this seasoned politician, who, even from jail, is giving chills to the old political guard in Pakistan. Such is his mass appeal and force of will that no earthly power can stop him in his moral crusade for truth and reform, except perhaps the Will of Allah.

As poetic philosopher Allama Iqbal immortalized in his epic 'Jawab-e-Shikwa':

> *"In this age, you are the vessel of Truth, the beacon*
> *for the lost wayfarer.*
> *For the unaware, your message signals the dawn of*
> *awareness.*
> *You think this chaos is merely worldly turmoil and*
> *temptation?*
> *Nay, it is a test of your resolve and sense of purpose.*
> *Why fret over attacks from ordinary mortals?*
> *The Light of Truth can never be extinguished by*
> *such schemes.*

Though hidden from the public eye, your reality is profound.
The caravan of life still awaits your leadership.
Your passion alone breathes life into this age.
Yours is the vice-regency of destiny's design.
The hour of opportunity beckons, much work remains unfinished.
The Light of Divine Unity still remains incomplete in this world.
Burst free from these shackles like a blossoming bud!
Become a whirlwind that sweeps out the stale air in the gardens of nations!
Transform each particle with the ecstatic rhythm of your convictions!
With the power of love lift up every downtrodden soul!
Fill this earth with the Light of Muhammad's Name!"

I conclude this book with the belief that though the path ahead is fraught with adversity, truth and justice shall ultimately prevail under the gallant leadership of Khan.

ABOUT THE AUTHOR

Emily is an acclaimed author and women's rights activist. She is the writer of a bestselling novel which chronicles the story of adversity and fight for women's rights.

Emily is also the author of two children's books. Her new book "Imran Khan - A Seasoned Politician" sheds light on the life and political career of the former Prime Minister of Pakistan.

In 2020, Emily was nominated for an award for her work empowering women. She made history as the first female author from her region to gain international recognition.

Emily continues to write influential books while advocating for women's education and rights. She is an inspiration for young women by showing them their boundless potential.